THE ART OF PROGRAMMING THROUGH FLOWCHARTS & ALGORITHMS

The Art of Programming Through Flowcharts & Algorithms

By

Anil Bikas Chaudhuri

Techno India Group
Head, Academic Divisions
The Institute of Computer Engineers (I)
Kolkata

FIREWALL MEDIA
(An Imprint of Laxmi Publications Pvt.Ltd.)
An ISO 9001:2015 Company

BENGALURU • CHENNAI • GUWAHATI • HYDERABAD • JALANDHAR
KOCHI • KOLKATA • LUCKNOW • MUMBAI • RANCHI
NEW DELHI

THE ART OF PROGRAMMING THROUGH FLOWCHARTS & ALGORITHMS

Printed and bound in India
Typeset at : Goswami Associates, Delhi
First Edition : 2005, *Reprint* : 2008, 2011, 2018, *Edition* : 2021
ISBN : 978-81-7008-779-3

Branches

Bengaluru	080-26 75 69 30
Chennai	044-24 34 47 26
Guwahati	0361-254 36 69
Hyderabad	040-27 55 53 83
Jalandhar	0181-222 12 72
Kochi	0484-405 13 03
Kolkata	033-40 04 77 79
Lucknow	0522-430 36 13
Ranchi	0651-224 24 64

PUBLISHED IN INDIA BY

FIREWALL MEDIA
(An Imprint of Laxmi Publications Pvt.Ltd.)

An ISO 9001:2015 Company
113, GOLDEN HOUSE, GURUDWARA ROAD, DARYAGANJ
NEW DELHI-110002, INDIA
Telephone : 91-11-4353 2500, 4353 2501
www.laxmipublications.com
info@laxmipublications.com

C—00001/021/07
Printed at: Repro Book Limited, Mumbai.

Preface

The inspiration for this book has come to me from my students who requested me many times to write such a book so that other students can grasp the art of program logic development easily and quickly. The book is aimed at inculcating problem solving skills among the beginners in computing science who are found to be ill-prepared to handle the problem-solving aspects of the discipline.

Although no book can be claimed to be self-contained, an attempt has been made to equip the readers with all the best followed, efficient, well-structured program logics in the form of flowcharts and algorithms. The illustrative examples will definitely encourage and enable students to solve the problems in the exercises and they will enjoy the task as a fun. As the task of logic development is an art, the same problem can be solved in a large number of ways; so the self-starters may try different logical approaches to the solutions or the instructors may guide the readers to redevelop the solutions in different approaches.

Suggestions for improvement of this work will be highly appreciated.

ANIL BIKAS CHAUDHURI

Acknowledgments

I would like to express my deepest gratitude to Mr. Gautam Roy Chowdhury, Chairman and Managing Director of Techno India Group, and to Mr. Tapan Kumar Ghosh, Chief Executive Officer of Techno India Group, to give me the opportunity to write text books for the students of their institute "The Institute of Computer Engineers (I)". It is through these projects I came to realise that I can write something for others—the self-confidence that made me bold enough to take over this project.

I am also grateful to Ms. Jayati Ghosh Dastidar, my ex-student and now colleague, who spent much of her valuable time to go through the manuscript patiently in finding out the omissions and commissions. I sincerely thank all my colleagues, friends and students who have appreciated this venture.

Contents

1 INTRODUCING TO PROGRAMMING

INTRODUCTION

A computer program is a sequential set of instructions written in some computer language that is used to direct the computer to perform some specific task of computation.

Observe that the definition demands that any set of instructions must be such that the tasks will, usually, be performed sequentially unless directed otherwise. Each instruction in the set will express a unit of work that a computer language can support. In general, high level languages, also known as 3GLs, support one human activity at a time. For example, if a computational task involves the determination of the average of three numbers, then it will require at least three human activities, *viz.*, getting the numbers, obtaining the sum of the numbers and then obtaining the average. So the process will require three instructions in a computer language. However, it can be done in two instructions also. First obtaining the numbers and second obtaining the sum and the average.

The objective of programming is problem-solving through computers speedily and accurately.

FLOWCHARTING AND ALGORITHM

A problem is something the result of which is not readily available. A set of steps involving arithmetic computation and/or logical manipulation is required to obtain the desired result. There is a law called the **law of equifinality** that states that the same goal can be achieved through different courses of action and a variety of paths. So the same result can be derived through a number of ways. For example, consider the task of sending a message to one of your friends. There are many ways in which this can be done. Firstly, you can convey the message over telephone, if your friend possesses some telephone connection. Secondly, your can send it by post ; thirdly, you can send it through some courier service and so on. If the message is urgent then you will try to use the quickest means in sending it. If it is not urgent then you will choose to send it in the least expensive but most reliable way of doing it. So depending upon the urgency, you will decide the best effective way of doing it. This best effective way is called the optimum way. The different ways of solving a problem are called solution strategies. The optimum way of solving a problem to get the desired result can be achieved by analysing different strategies for the solution and then selecting the way that can yield the result in the least time using minimum resources. The selection process will depend on the efficiency of the person and his/her understanding of the problem. He/she must also be familiar with different problem-solving techniques. Determining the set of steps required to solve a given problem is an art. It shows how decently a person can arrange a set of steps so that others can follow it and that too with a high degree of dexterity. So an analysis called 'task analysis' is required to reach the solution from 'problem definition' that states what is to be achieved.

A set of steps that generates a finite sequence of elementary computational operations leading to the solution of a given problem is called an **algorithm.** An algorithm may be too verbose to follow. The textual description of an algorithm may not be understood by all easily and quickly. This is why a pictorial representation may be used as a substitute of an algorithm. Such a pictorial representation is called a flowchart. Formally speaking, a flowchart is a diagrammatic representation of the steps of an algorithm. In a flowchart, boxes of different shapes are used to denote different types of operations. These boxes are then connected by lines with arrowheads denoting the flow or direction to which one should proceed to know the next step. The connecting lines are known as flow lines. Flowcharts may be classified into two categories :

(*i*) Program Flowchart (*ii*) System Flowchart.

Program flowcharts act like mirrors of computer programs in terms of flowcharting symbols. They contain the steps of solving a problem unit for a specific result.

System flowcharts, on the contrary, contain solution of many problem units together that are closely related to each other and interact with each other to achieve a goal. We shall first focus on program flowcharts.

A **program flowchart** is an extremely useful tool in program development activity in many respects. Firstly, any error, omission or commission can be easily detected from a program flowchart than it can be from a program because a program flowchart is a pictorial representation of the logic of a program. Secondly, a program flowchart can be followed easily and quickly. Thirdly, it serves as a good document, which may be of great help if the need for program modification arises in future.

The following five rules should be followed while drawing program flowcharts.

- Only the standard symbols should be used in program flowcharts.
- A program logic should depict the flow from top to bottom and from left to right.
- Each symbol used in a program flowchart should contain only one entry point and one exit point, with the exception of the decision symbol. This is known as the 'single' rule.
- The operations shown within a symbol of a program flowchart should be expressed independent of any particular programming language.
- All decision branches should be well-labeled.

The following are the standard symbols used in program flowcharts :

Terminal. Used to show the beginning and end of a set of computer-related process.

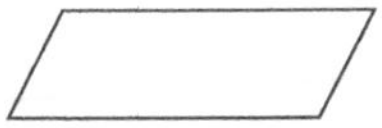

Input/Output. Used to show any Input/Output operation.

Computer processing. Used to show any processing performed by a computer system.

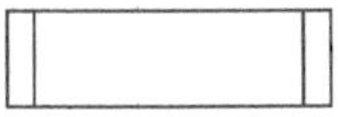

Predefined processing. Used to indicate any process not specially defined in the flowchart.

Comment. Used to write any explanatory statement required to clarify something.

Flow line. Used to connect the symbols.

Document Input/Output. Used when input comes from a document and output goes to a document.

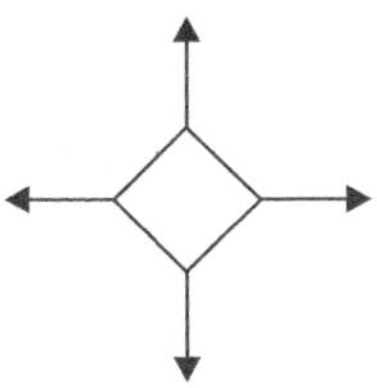

Decision. Used to show any point in the process where a decision must be made to determine futher action.

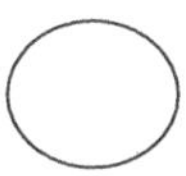

On-page connector. Used to connect parts of a flowchart continued on the same page.

Off-page connector. Used to connect parts of a flowchart continued to separate pages.

Flowcharts can be used to show the sequence of steps for doing any job. A set of simple operations involving accepting inputs, performing arithmetic operation on the inputs and showing them to the users demonstrate the SEQUENCE logic structure of a program. The following flowchart shows the steps in cooking rice and then utilising the cooked rice.

Algorithm for the flowchart given on next page will be as follows :

Step 1. Take the rice to be cooked

Step 2. Procure the container

Step 3. Procure water

Step 4. Wash the rice in water

Step 5. Put the rice in the container

Step 6. Pour water into the container

Step 7. IF WATER LEVEL = 1 INCH ABOVE THE RICE
    THEN GOTO STEP 8
    ELSE GOTO STEP 6
  ENDIF

This is illustrated below :

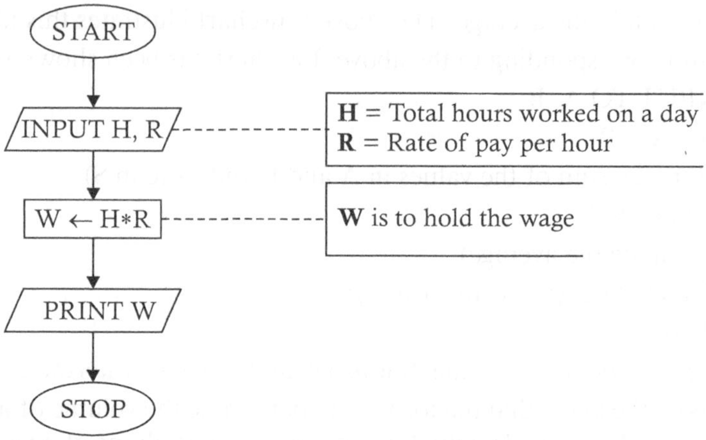

The algorithm for the solution of the above problem is given below :

Step 1. INPUT TO H, R

Step 2. COMPUTE W ← H *R

(Store the product of the values in H and R in W)

Stop 3. PRINT W

Stop 4. STOP

Problem 1.5. *Construct a flowchart to show how to obtain the area of a triangle on the basis of base and altitude.*

Task Analysis. We know that the formula to find out the area of a triangle is :

$$\text{Area} = \frac{1}{2} \times \text{base} \times \text{altitude}$$

So the inputs required to obtain the area of a triangle are its base and height *i.e.*, altitude. We can then put the values in the above formula to obtain the area.

This is illustrated below :

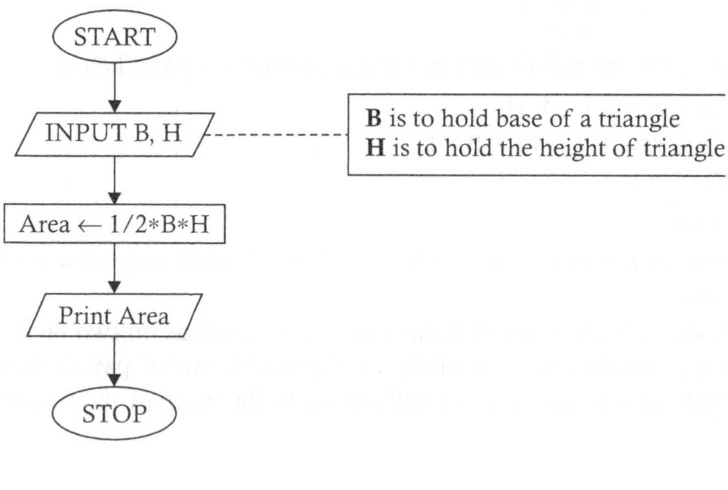

The algorithm corresponding to the above procedure is given below :

Step 1. INPUT TO B, H

(B is for base and H is for height of triangle)

Step 2. COMPUTE AREA $\leftarrow \frac{1}{2} * B * H$

Step 3. PRINT AREA

Step 4. STOP.

Problem 1.6. *Develop a flowchart to show the steps in finding out the simple interest on a given amount at a given rate of interest.*

Task Analysis. We know that if P be the principal, R be the rate of interest and T be the term in years then the simple interest I is given by the formula $I = \frac{P * R * T}{100}$. So to determine the simple interest on a given amount, we need the principal amount (P), the rate of interest (R) and the term in years (T). By putting the values in the formula above, we get the desired simple interest.

The flowchart is illustrated below :

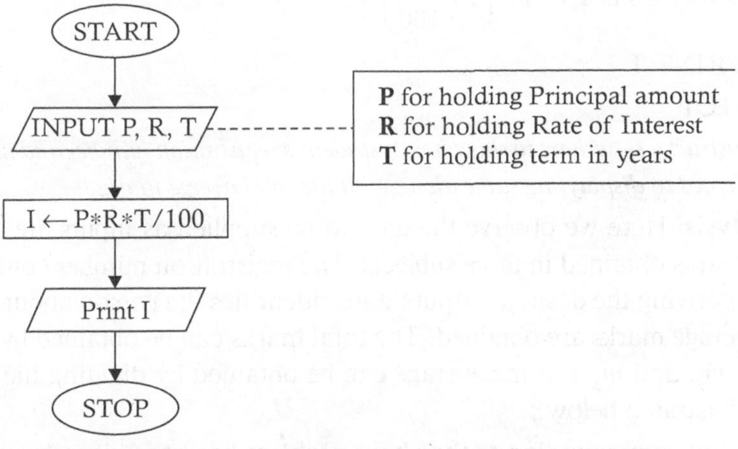

The algorithm corresponding to the above logic is given below :

Step 1. INPUT TO P, R, T

Step 2. COMPUTE $I \leftarrow P * R * T / 100$

Step 3. PRINT I

Step 4. STOP

Problem 1.7. *If P amount of money is invested for N years at an annual rate of interest I, the money grows to an amount T where T is given by :* $T = P(1 + I/100)^N$. *Draw a flowchart to show how T is determined.*

Task Analysis. The solution to this problem is very simple (straight forward) and it is similar to the preceding one. The inputs required are values for P, I and N. The output T can then be obtained by putting the values in the formula.

This is illustrated below :

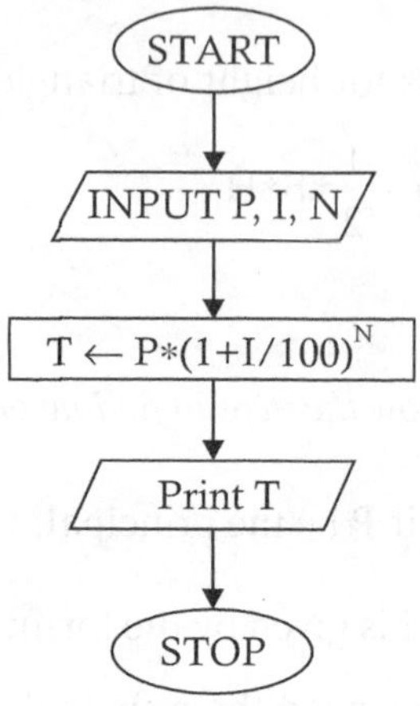

The algorithm corresponding to the above flowchart is given below :

Step 1. INPUT TO P, I, N

Step 2. COMPUTE $T \leftarrow P^* \left(1 + \frac{I}{100}\right)^N$

Step 3. PRINT T

Step 4. STOP

Problem 1.8. *Construct a flowchart to show how a student's registration number and marks in 3 subjects m_1, m_2, m_3 are accepted to display the same along with the total averge marks.*

Task Analysis. Here we observe the data to be supplied as inputs are : (*i*) registration number and (*ii*) marks obtained in three subjects. The registration number contributes nothing in the process of deriving the desired output ; it just identifies the person about whom the total marks and the average marks are obtained. The total marks can be obtained by taking the sum of the marks m_1, m_2, and m_3 and the average can be obtained by dividing the total by 3. The steps have been illustrated below :

The algorithm corresponding to the above problem has been given below :

Step 1. INPUT TO REGN-NO

Step 2. INPUT TO M1, M2, M3

(M1, M2 and M3 are for holding marks of three subjects)

Step 3. COMPUTE T ← M1 + M2 + M3

Step 4. COMPUTE AVG ← T/3

Step 5. PRINT REGN-NO, AVG

Step 6. STOP.

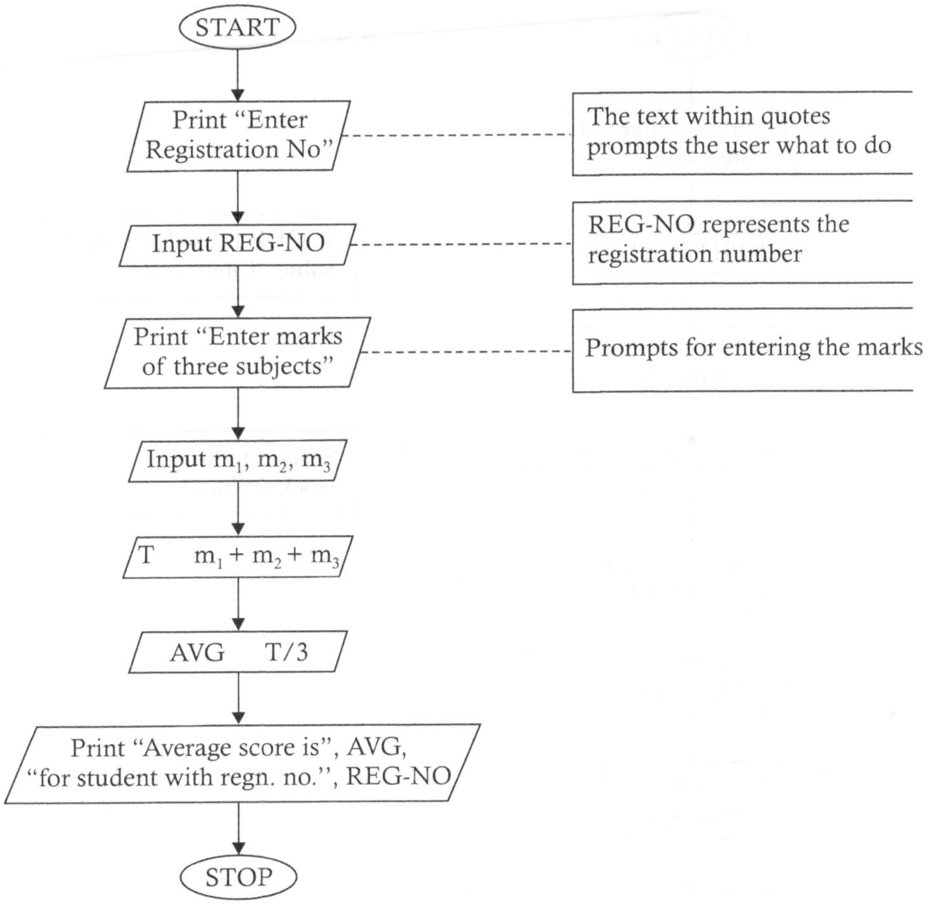

Problem 1.9. *Draw a flowchart to accept the item-code, stock on hand and the rate per unit stock in a departmental store and display the stock value of the store.*

Task Analysis. The inputs required to determine the stock value of the stores are clearly the stock on hand and the rate per unit stock which are to be multiplied together to determine the stock value. The item-code is used as an identification data. The flowchart has been shown below :

The algorithm corresponding to the solution given on next page has been shown below :

Step 1. INPUT TO I CODE

Step 2. INPUT TO SOH (SOH stands for stock on hand)

Step 3. INPUT TO RATE

Step 4. COMPUTE STOCK-VALUE ←SOH * RATE

Step 5. PRINT STOCK-VALUE, ICODE

Step 6. STOP.

ELSE
COMPUTE L ← CP – SP
PRINT "LOSS IS"; L
END-IF

Step 3. STOP

Problem 2.2. *Construct a procedure to show how to determine the greater number of two given numbers.*

Task Analysis. Note that we are required to determine the larger between two given numbers. So there is a task of decision-making to compare the given numbers to find out the greater of them.

This is illustrated below :

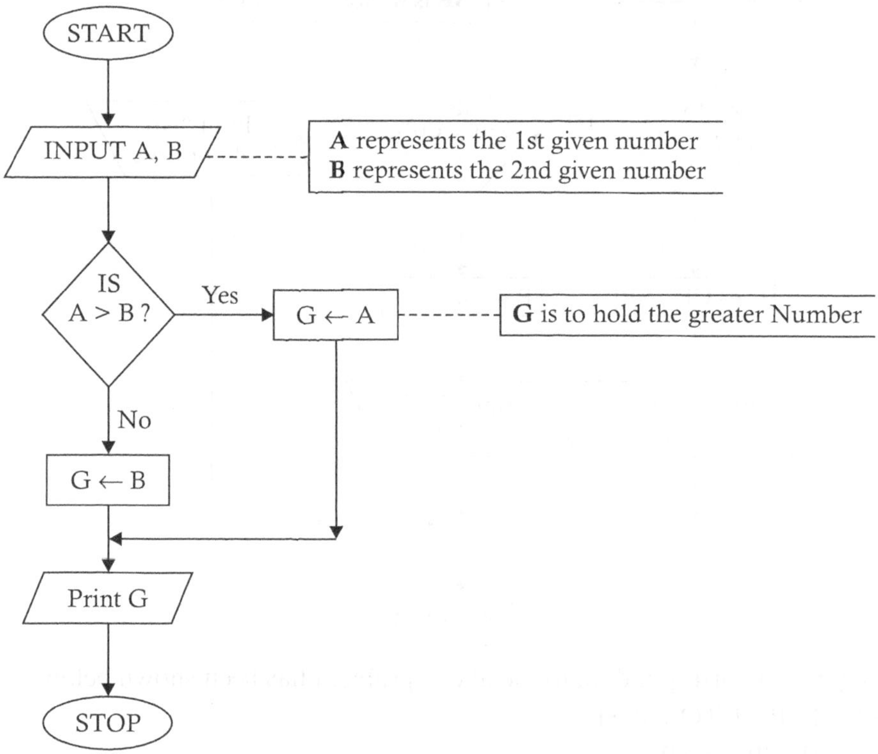

Note. Here we have assumed that the given numbers are different numbers.

The algorithm corresponding to the above problem has been given below :

Step 1. INPUT TO A, B

Step 2. IF A > B
THEN G ← A
ELSE
G ← B
END-IF

Step 3. PRINT G

Step 4. STOP

Problem 2.3. *Construct a flowchart to determine whether a given number is even or odd.*

Task Analysis. From the concept of mathematics, we know that a given number is called an even number if it is completely divisible by 2. This means that if we perform integer division upon the given number then the remainder of the division will be zero. So, to construct the flowchart we shall accept a number as input, obtain the remainder of integer division by taking 2 as divisor and then we shall check whether the remainder is zero or not. If it is zero, then our conclusion will be that the number is an even number, otherwise, it will be an odd number.

The above logic is depicted in the flowchart below :

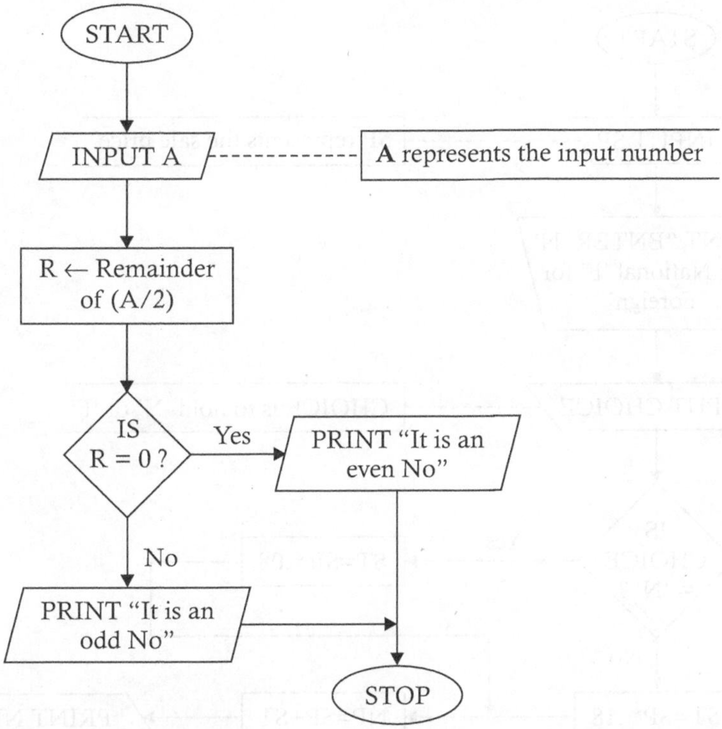

The algorithm corresponding to the above flowchart has been shown below :

Step 1. INPUT TO A

Step 2. COMPUTE R ← Remainder of (A/2)

Step 3. IF R = 0

THEN PRINT "It is an even No."

ELSE

PRINT "It is an odd No."

END-IF

Step 4. STOP.

Problem 2.4. *It is required to determine the net payable amount on a sale. The net payable amount consists of sale price plus sales tax. The sales tax is decided as under :*

(a) 8% of sale price for national items.

(b) 18% of sale price for foreign items.

Construct a flowchart to show how the net payable amount is determined.

Task Analysis. It is clear from the problem that we are required to calculate sales tax first by taking one of the two given rates. For this purpose, we require two inputs. First, the sale price of the item under consideration, second, the origin of the item. Let us assume that we shall provide 'N' or 'F' as input to indicate national or foreign respectively. The following flowchart shows this :

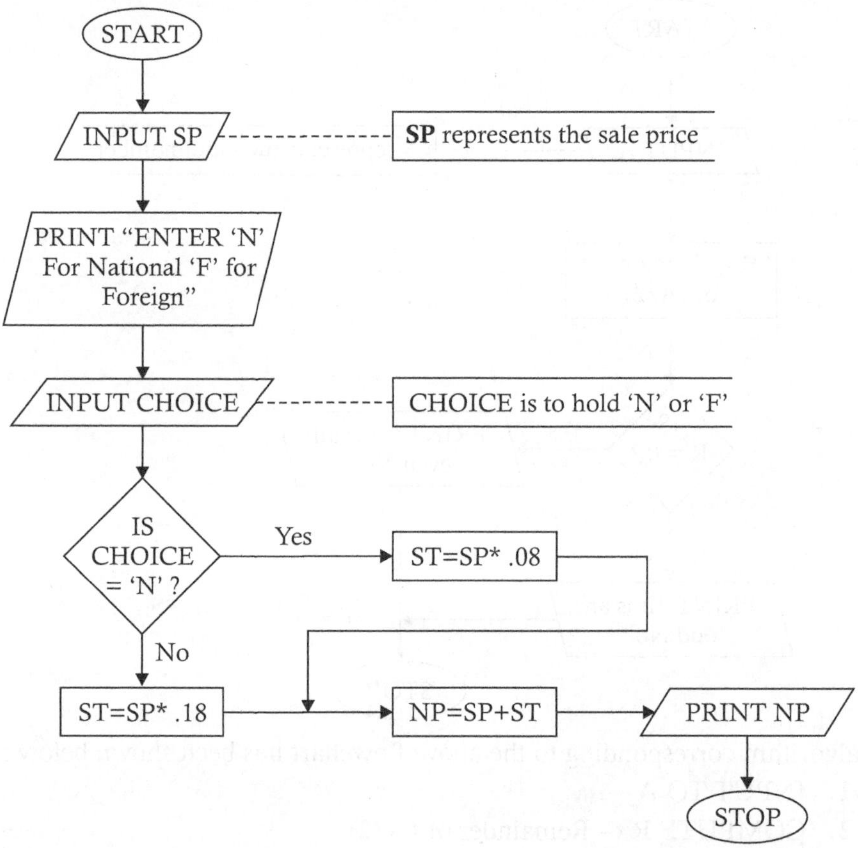

The algorithm corresponding to the above solution has been shown below :

Step 1. INPUT TO SP

Step 2. INPUT TO CHOICE ('N' for national and 'F' for foreign)

Step 3. IF CHOICE = 'N'

THEN COMPUTE ST ← SP∗.08

ELSE

COMPUTE ST ← SP*.18
END-IF
COMPUTE NP ← NP+ST

Step 4. PRINT NP
Step 5. STOP

Problem 2.5. *An equation of the form $ax^2 + bx + c = 0$ is known as quadratic equation. Draw a flowchart to show how to solve a quadratic equation.*

Task Analysis. Note that the values a, b and c in the given equation represent constant values. So $4x^2 - 17x - 15 = 0$ represents a quadratic equation where $a = 4$, $b = -17$ and $c = -15$. The values of x that satisfy a particular quadratic equation, are known as the roots of the equation. The roots may be calculated by substituting the values of a, b and c into the following two formulas :

$$x_1 = (-b + \sqrt{b^2 - 4ac})/2a$$
$$x_2 = (-b - \sqrt{b^2 - 4ac})/2a$$

The expression $b^2 - 4ac$ is called the determinant of the equation because it determines the nature of the roots of the equation. If the value of the determinant is less than zero, then the roots of the equation x_1 and x_2, are imaginary (complex) numbers. So to solve a quadratic equation, we should allow the user to enter the values for a, b and c. If the discriminant is less than zero, then a message should be displayed stating that the roots are imaginary ; otherwise the program should proceed to calculate and display the two roots of the equation. The steps are shown in the following flowchart :

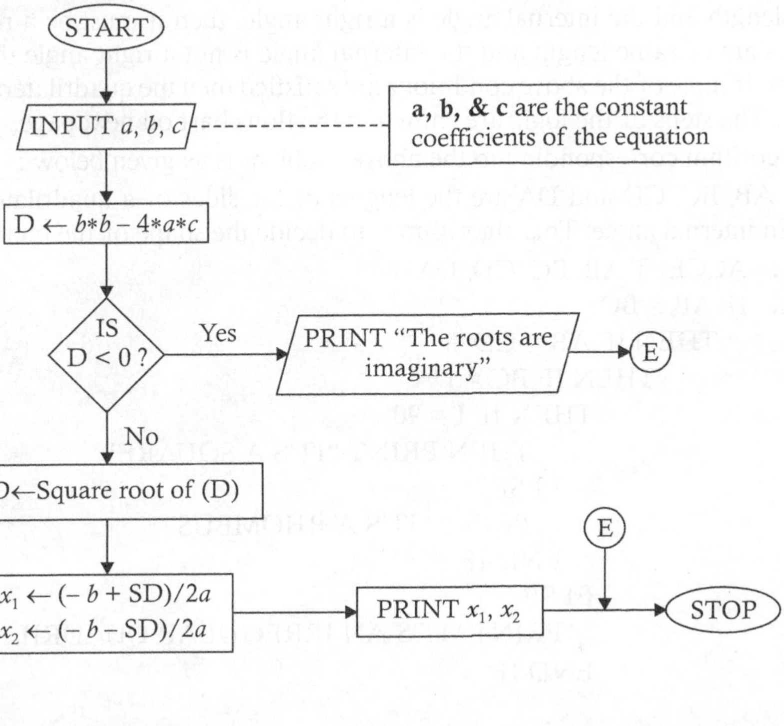

The algorithm corresponding to the above program is as follows :

```
Step 1.  INPUT TO A, B, C
Step 2.  COMPUTE D ← (B*B – 4*A*C) (Calculate the value of the discriminant) and
         store in D
Step 3.  IF D < 0
            THEN PRINT "THE ROOTS ARE IMAGINARY"
         ELSE
            COMPUTE SD ← SQUARE-ROOT (D)
         END-IF
Step 4.  COMPUTE X1 ← (– b + SD)/2*A
Step 5.  COMPUTE X2 ← (– b – SD)/2*A
Step 6.  PRINT X1, X2
Step 7.  STOP
```

Problem 2.6. *Write a program to categorise the shape of a quadrilateral as either a square, rhombus, rectangle, parallelogram or irregular quadrilateral, having input the lengths of the four sides and one internal angle.*

Task Analysis. Observe that to take decision about the shape of a quadrilateral, we are required to know the definitions of the quadrilaterals. A quadrilateral is called a square, if all the sides are of equal length and each of the internal angles is a right angle. A quadrilateral is called rhombus if the lengths of all sides are same and no angle is a right angle. So if only one internal angle is given and the sides are given, then in case all sides are of same length and the internal angle is not a right angle then the quadrilateral must be a rhombus. If the internal angle is a right angle and the sides are of same length then it must be a square. If the opposide sides are of same length and the internal angle is a right angle, then it must be a rectangle ; if the opposite sides are of same length and the internal angle is not a right angle then it must be a parallelogram. If none of the above conditions are satisfied then the quadrilateral is an irregular quadrilateral. The steps of the logic are shown in the flowchart on next page.

The algorithm corresponding to the above problem is as given below :

Given AB, BC, CD and DA are the lengths of the sides of a quadrilateral and I is the measure of an internal angle. This algorithm is to decide the shape of the quadrilateral.

```
Step 1.  ACCEPT AB, BC, CD, DA, I
Step 2.  IF AB = BC
            THEN IF AB = CD
                THEN IF BC = DA
                    THEN IF I = 90
                        THEN PRINT "IT'S A SQUARE"
                      ELSE
                        PRINT "IT'S A RHOMBUS"
                      END-IF
                    ELSE
                      PRINT "IT'S AN IRREGULAR QUADRILATERAL"
                    END-IF
```

```
            ELSE
                PRINT "IT'S AN IRREGULAR QUADRILATERAL"
            END-IF
        ELSE
            IF AB = CD
            THEN IF BC = DA
                    THEN IF I = 90
                            THEN PRINT "IT'S A RECTANGLE"
                         ELSE
                            PRINT "IT'S A PARALLELOGRAM"
                         END-IF
                 ELSE
                    PRINT "IT'S AN IRREGULAR QUADRILATERAL"
                 END-IF
            ELSE
                PRINT "IT'S AN IRREGULAR QUADRILATERAL"
        END-IF
```

Step 3. STOP

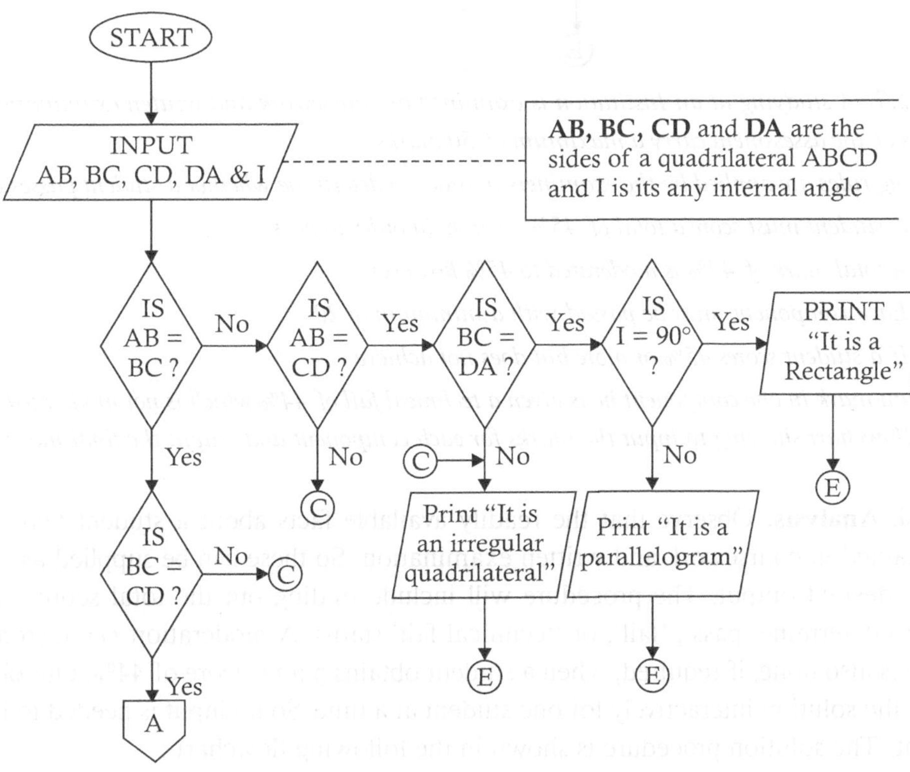

```
Step 3. IF MCW > 20
            THEN IF MWE > 20
                    THEN IF TOT > 45
                            THEN RESULT ← "PASS"
                                    (Store 'PASS' in RESULT)
                            ELSE
                              IF TOT = 44
                                    THEN RESULT ← 45
                                      (Moderation of 44 to make it 45)
                                        RESULT ← "PASS"
                              ELSE
                                    RESULT ← "FAIL"
                              END-IF
                                END-IF
                            ELSE
                              IF TOT ≥ 45
                                THEN
                                    TOT ← 44
                                    RESULT ← "TECHNICAL FAIL"
                              END-IF
                            END-IF
                    ELSE
                      IF MWE > 20
                        THEN
                        TOT ← 44
                            RESULT ← "TECHNICAL FAIL"
                      END-IF
        END-IF
Step 4. PRINT TOT, RESULT
Step 5. STOP
```

Problem 2.8. *The following rules are used to calculate bonus for employees of an organization.*

(i) If pay is more than Rs. 3000 the bonus amount is fixed and it is equal to Rs. 300.

(ii) If pay is more than Rs. 1600 but less than or equal to Rs. 3000, the bonus will be 10% of pay subject to a maximum of Rs. 240.

(iii) If pay is less than or equal to Rs. 1600, the bonus is 15% of pay, subject to a minimum of Rs. 100.

Task Analysis. Obviously, the input required here is the pay amount that an employee gets. On the basis of the pay, we can determine the bonus amount. The "subject to maximum" or the "subject to minimum" clause implies that the calculated amount is to be compared with the maximum or minimum limit, if it is more than the maximum limit or less than the minimum limit, then the maximum limit or the minimum limit will be treated as the legitimate value. This is illustrated below.

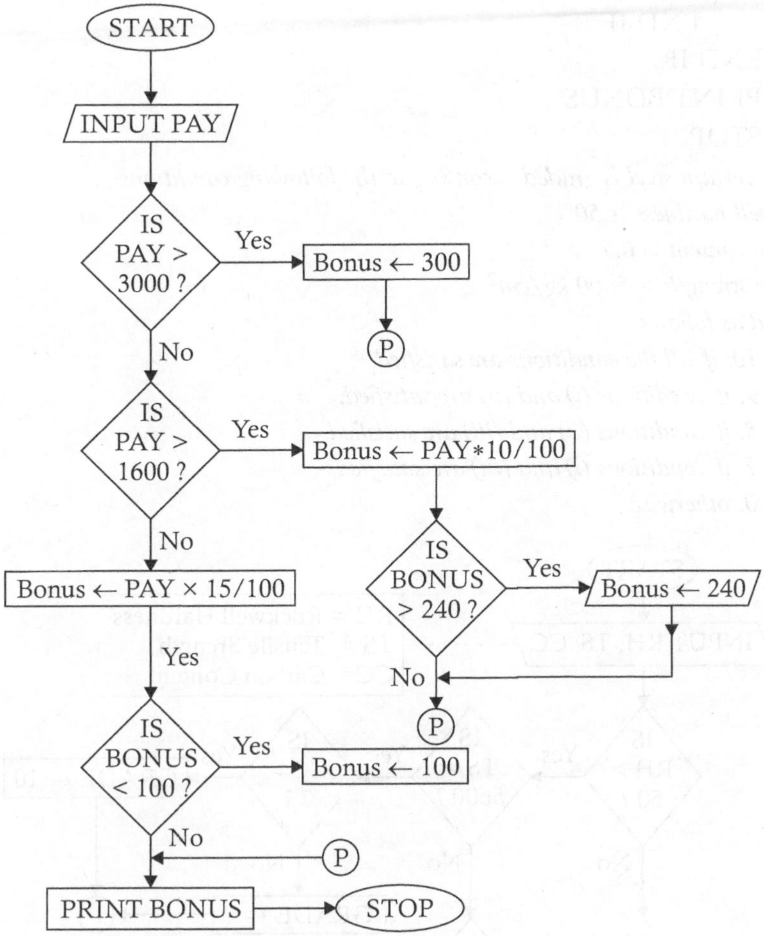

The algorithm corresponding to the above problem has been given below :

Step 1. INPUT TO PAY

Step 2. IF PAY > 3000

```
THEN BONUS ← 300
ELSE
   IF PAY > 1600
      THEN BONUS ← PAY*10/100
           IF BONUS > 240
              THEN
                    BONUS ← 240
           END-IF
      ELSE
         BONUS ← PAY*15/100
           IF BONUS < 100
              BONUS ← 100
           END-IF
```

END-IF
END-IF
Step 3. PRINT BONUS
Step 4. STOP

Problem 2.9. *A certain steel is graded according to the following conditions :*

(i) Rockwell hardness > 50
(ii) Carbon content > 0.7
(iii) Tensile strength > 5600 kg/cm^2

The steel is graded as follows :

(a) Grade 10, if all the conditions are satisfied.
(b) Grade 9, if conditions (i) and (ii) are satisfied.
(c) Grade 8, if conditions (ii) and (iii) are satisfied.
(d) Grade 7, if conditions (i) and (iii) are satisfied.
(e) Grade 0, otherwise.

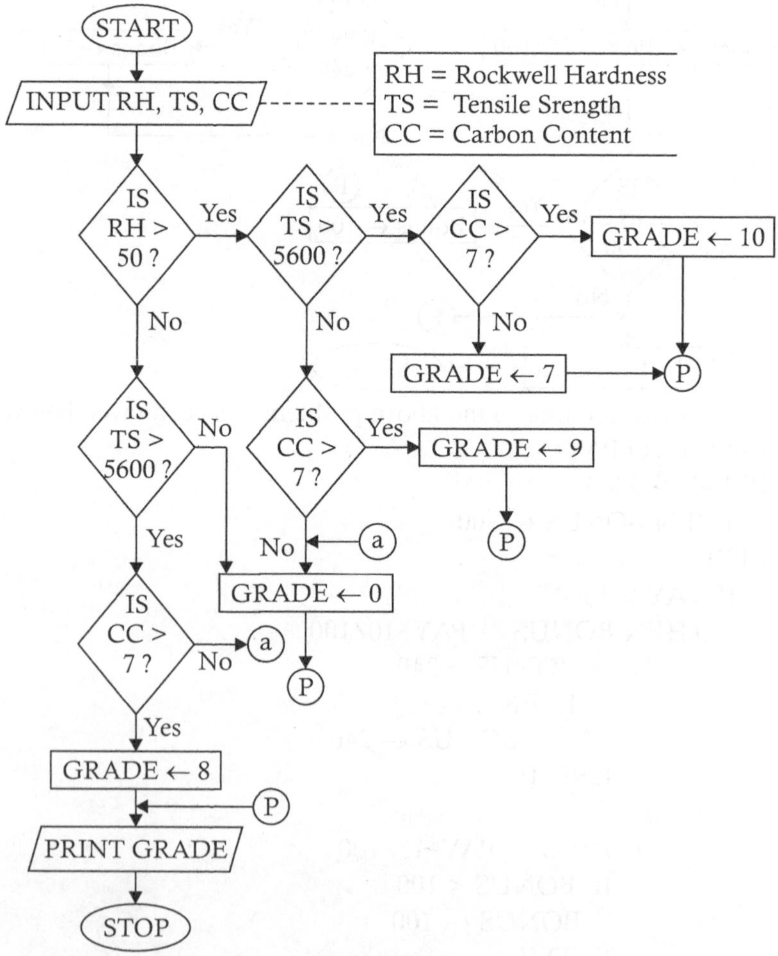

Step 3. PRINT "THE GREATEST OF THE GIVEN NOS. IS :", G

Step 4. STOP

Problem 2.11. *A bookseller offers two rates of commissions. If the price of a book lies below 100, the rate of commission is 12% of the price, otherwise, it is 18% of the price. It is required to develop a procedure to determine the discount and the net price of a book.*

Task Analysis. Here we observe that the outputs required are discount and net price of a book. The only input required for the purpose is price of the book. The rates of discount are constants (fixed). So these rates can be used to form formulas to calculate discounts in the two different cases. The calculated discount can then be subtracted from the price of the book to obtain the net price. The procedure is illustrated though the following flowchart :

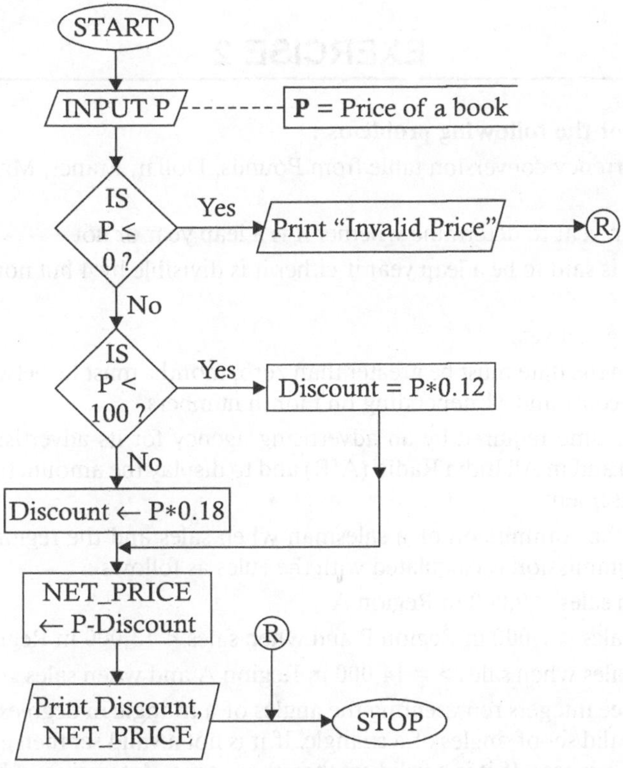

Note that the procedure suggests the printing of a message when some absurd input is provided.

The algorithm corresponding to the above problem has been given below :

Step 1. INPUT TO P
(Accept the price of a book in P)

Step 2. IF P <= 0
THEN PRINT "INVALID PRICE"

```
         ELSE
            IF P < 100
         COMPUTE D ← P*0.12 (Store the calculated discount in D)
            ELSE
         COMPUTE D ← P*0.18
            END-IF
         END-IF
Step 3.  COMPUTE NET_PRICE ← P – D
Step 4.  PRINT D, NET_PRICE
Step 5.  STOP
```

EXERCISE 2

Construct flowcharts for the following problems :

(*i*) To print a currency conversion table from Pounds, Dollar, Francs, Marks and Lire to Indian Rupees.

(*ii*) To test a given year to determine whether it is a leap year or not.

Hint. A year is said to be a leap year if either it is divisible by 4 but not by 100 or divisible by 400.

(*iii*) To validate a given year.

Hints. Year in the date must be greater than zero, months must lie between 1 and 12 and days must lie between 1 and 31 depending on month numbers.

(*iv*) To accept the time required by an advertising agency for its advertising program to run in Doordarshan and in All India Radio (AIR) and to display the amount to be paid by the agency for its advertisement.

(*v*) To calculate the commission of a salesman when sales and the region of sales are given as input. The commission is calculated with the rules as follows :

(a) Nil, when sales < 9,000 in Region A

(b) 5.5% of sales < 7,000 in Region B and when sales < 13,000 in Region A

(c) 7.5% of sales when sales > = 14,000 in Region A and when sales > = 13,000 in Region B.

(*vi*) To accept three integers representing the angles of a triangle in degrees to determine whether they form a valid set of angles of a triangle. If it is not a valid set then generate a message and terminate the process. If it is a valid set then the process determines whether it is equiangular (all three angles are same). It also determines if the triangle is right angled (has one angle with 90 degrees), obtuse angled (One angle above 90), or acute (all three angles are below 90 degrees) angled. Finally it shows conclusion about the triangle.

(*vii*) To accept the length of three sides of a triangle to validate whether they can be the sides of a triangle and then classify the triangle as equilateral (all three sides are equal) scalene (all three sides are different) or isosceles (exactly two sides are equal) and then to see whether it is a right angled triangle (the sum of the squares of two sides is equal to the square of the third side.)

Hint. Three numbers are valid as the sides of a triangle if each one is positive and the sum of every two numbers is greater than the third.

(*viii*) To allow the user to perform a simple task on a calculator on the basis of a given choice as follows :

+, −, ×, / or % representing usual arithmetic operators

A	Average of two nos.
X	Maximum of two nos.
M	Minimum of two nos.
S	Square of two nos.
Q	Quit

(*ix*) An electricity board charges the following rates to domestic users to discourage large consumption of energy :

for the first 100 units—85 p per unit

for the next 200 units—Rs. 1.45 per unit

Beyond 300 units—Rs. 1.85 per unit

All users are charged a minimum of Rs. 500.00. If the total cost is more than Rs. 2500.00, then an additional surcharge of 3% of the total cost is added to the total cost to determine the final bill.

(*x*) To determine and print the minimum number of currency notes of the denominations : Re. 1, Rs. 5, Rs. 10, Rs. 20, Rs. 50, Rs. 100, Rs. 500 and Rs. 1000 required to pay any given amount.

3 PROBLEMS ON LOOPING

INTRODUCTION

In the flowcharts of the preceding chapter we have demonstrated 'sequence' and 'selection' logic structures. Now let us demonstrate 'iteration' logic structure.

The term **iteration** means **repetition.** Sometimes, some procedure should be executed repeatedly. Truly speaking, all procedures should be built so that it can be repeated, as many times as needed. We do not develop procedures to execute only once but a number of times as required. Otherwise, calculators could be sufficient to obtain the results. An iterative logic structure is also known as a 'loop'. So 'looping' means repeating a set of operations to obtain some result again and again.

An iteration may be implemented in two ways namely, **pretest iteration and post-test iteration.** In case of a pretest iteration, a predicate is tested to decide whether a set of operations is to be performed or not. If the condition implied by the predicate is true, then the desired operations are performed, if it is false, then the iteration is terminated. This is shown in the following diagram.

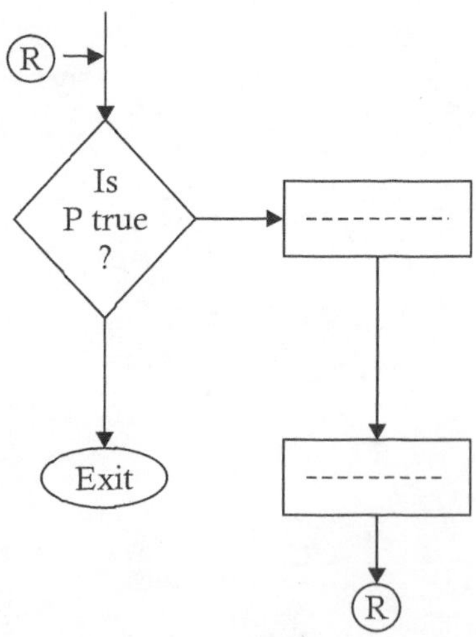

In case of a post-test iteration, the predicate is tested after performing a set of operations once to decide whether to repeat the set of operations or to terminate the repetition. If the condition happens to be true then the set of operations is repeated, otherwise, it is not repeated. The diagrammatic structure of this logic is as follows :

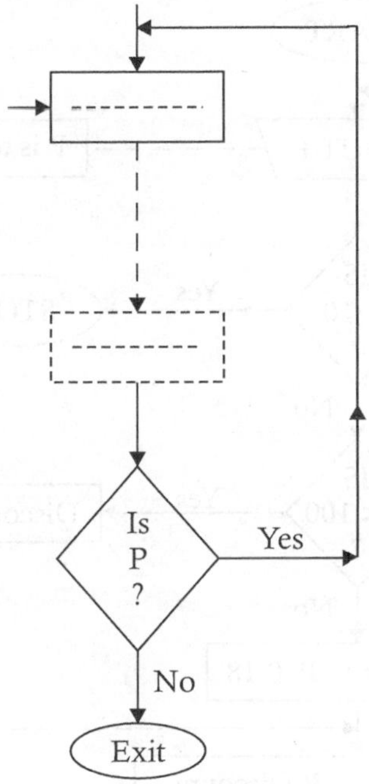

Note that the operations in the loop must be performed at least once in case of post-test iteration.

The concept of looping can be demonstrated in the following flowchart. Of course, there should be a condition for normal termination. Let us assume that the repetitive task of calculating discounts and net prices will be terminated, when we provide negative or zero price as input. Such absurd values are justified for termination of loops so that the procedure can remain valid for any possible value of price. We, usually, use out-connectors and in-connectors with the same label to demonstrate the end-point and start-point of a loop. This is shown for the flowchart of the problem 2.11.

The algorithm corresponding to the flowchart given on next page is as shown below :

Step 1. REPEAT STEPS 2 THROUGH 6 (Start Loop)

Step 2. INPUT TO P

Step 3. If $P \leq 0$ THEN EXIT (Stop Repetition *i.e.*, transfer the control to STOP).

Step 4. If $P < 100$

THEN COMPUTE $D \leftarrow P*0.12$

ELSE COMPUTE $D \leftarrow P*0.18$

END-IF

Step 5. COMPUTE NET_PRICE ← P – D
Step 6. PRINT D, NET_PRICE (End of loop)
Step 7. STOP

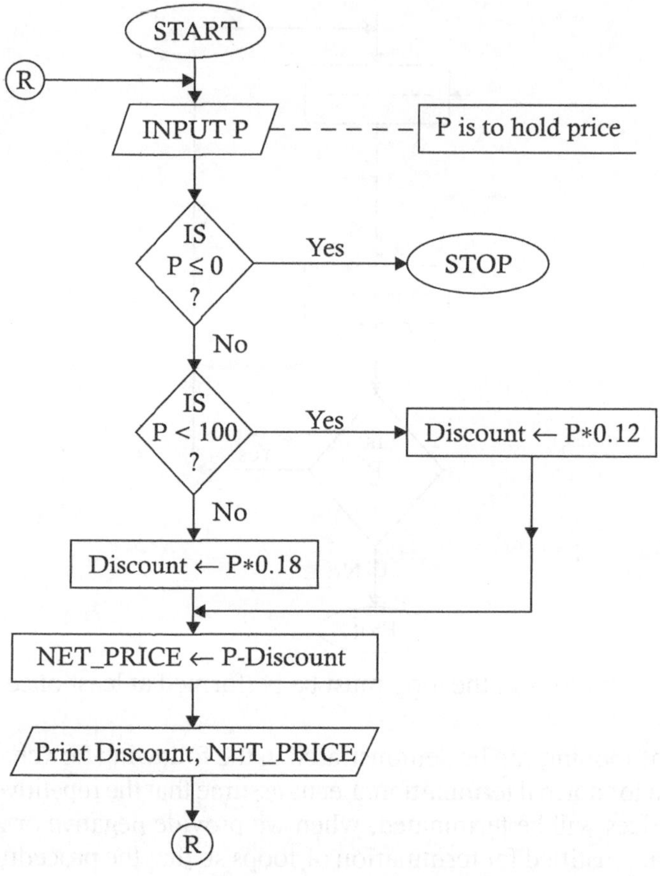

Note that the out-connector (R) shows the end-point of the loop and the in-connector. (R)→ shows the start-point of the loop. So the operations starting from the point of accepting input price upto the points of printing the outputs discount and net-price are within the loop. It could have been demonstrated in the following way also without using connectors.

But we prefer the preceding one to the following one, because if the flowchart cannot be accommodated in a single page or in a continuous structure on a single page it would be impossible or difficult or cumbersome to connect the start-point and the end-point.

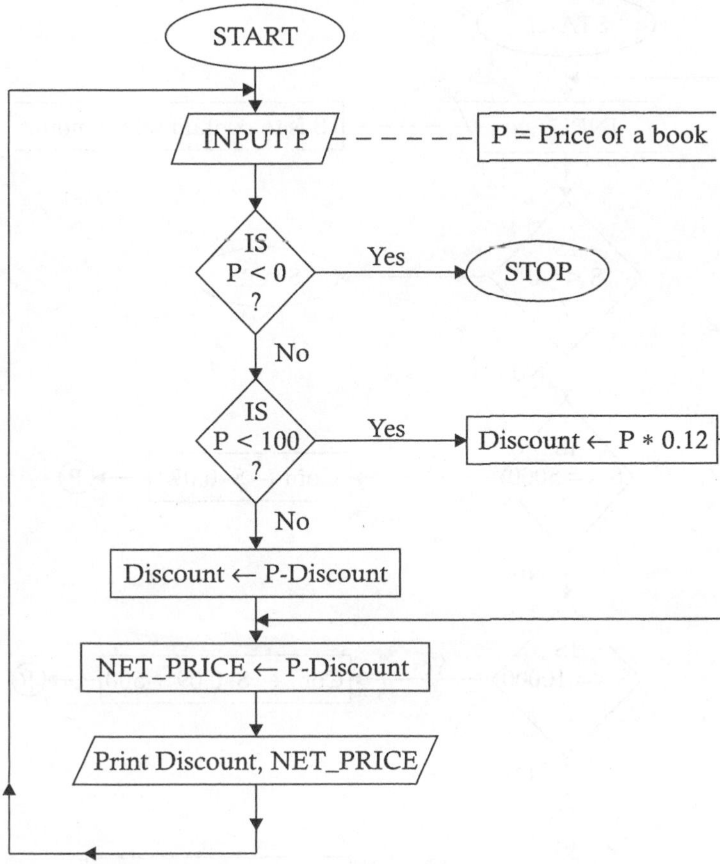

Problem 3.1. *The salesmen of a sales firm are given commission on sales achieved, according to the following rules :*

Sales	*Rate of commission*
<= 5,000	*7% of sales*
> 5,000 but <= 10,000	*9% of sales + Rs. 500*
> 10,000 but <= 20,000	*11% of sales + Rs. 1000*
> 20,000 but <= 25,000	*13% of sales + Rs. 2000*
> 25,000	*15% of sales + Rs. 4000*

It is required to devise a procedure to calculate the commission of the salesmen.

Task Analysis. Here the output required is the commission earned by a salesman. The only input required is the amount of sale achieved. A number of decision-making steps are involved here and the process is likely to be repeated a number of times. Let us assume that the process can be terminated when the amount of sale is given to be zero or negative. The procedure is illustrated in the following flowchart.

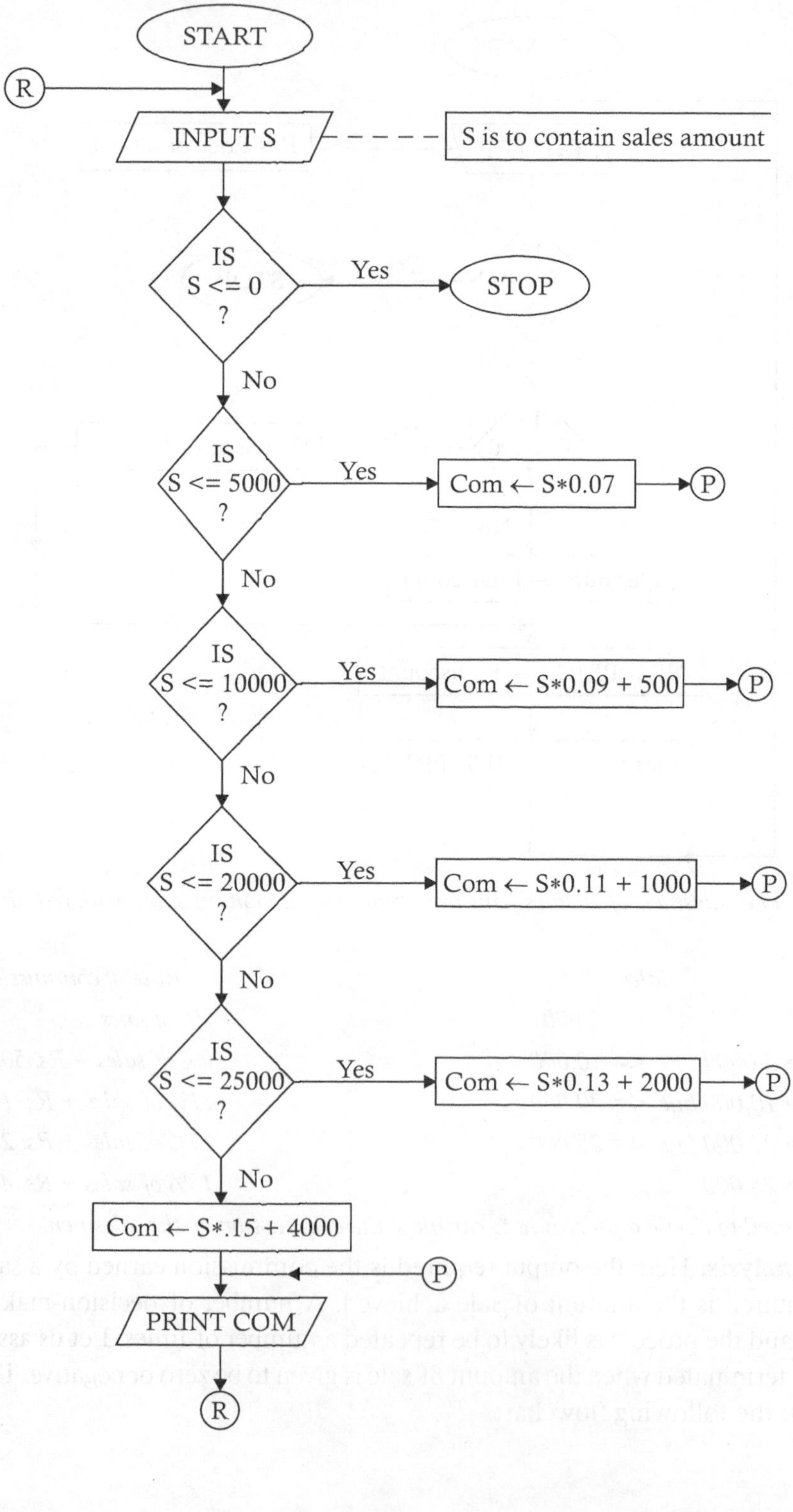
START
R
INPUT S
S is to contain sales amount
IS S <= 0 ?
Yes
STOP
No
IS S <= 5000 ?
Yes
Com ← S*0.07
P
No
IS S <= 10000 ?
Yes
Com ← S*0.09 + 500
P
No
IS S <= 20000 ?
Yes
Com ← S*0.11 + 1000
P
No
IS S <= 25000 ?
Yes
Com ← S*0.13 + 2000
P
No
Com ← S*.15 + 4000
P
PRINT COM
R

The algorithm corresponding to the above problem has been given below :

```
Step 1.  REPEAT STEPS 2 THROUGH 5
Step 2.  INPUT TO S
         (Accept sales amount in S)
Step 3.  If S <= 0
           THEN EXIT
         END-IF
Step 4.  IF S <= 5000
           THEN COMPUTE COM ← S * .07
         ELSE
           IF S <= 10000
             THEN COMPUTE COM ← S * .09 + 500
           ELSE
             IF S <= 20000
               THEN COMPUTE COM ← S * 0.11 + 1000
             ELSE
               IF S <= 25000
                 THEN COMPUTE COM ← S * 0.13 + 2000
               ELSE
                 COMPUTE COM ← S * 0.15 + 4000
               END-IF
             END-IF
           END-IF
         END-IF
Step 5.  PRINT COM
Step 6.  STOP
```

Problem 3.2. *A sales organization offers a fixed salary and a percentage of sales as commission to determine the monthly remuneration of an employee under the following condition.*

If the sales amount of an employee exceeds Rs. 5000 then the commission to be given is 12% of sales that exceeds 5000 otherwise it is nil.

Draw a flowchart to show how the remuneration of an employee is decided.

Task Analysis. Here we note that the remuneration of an employee consists of two parts, namely, a fixed salary part and a commission part that depends on sales amount. So we are to know the fixed salary part and the sales amount as input to determine the commission and hence the remuneration. The procedure can be illustrated as follows :

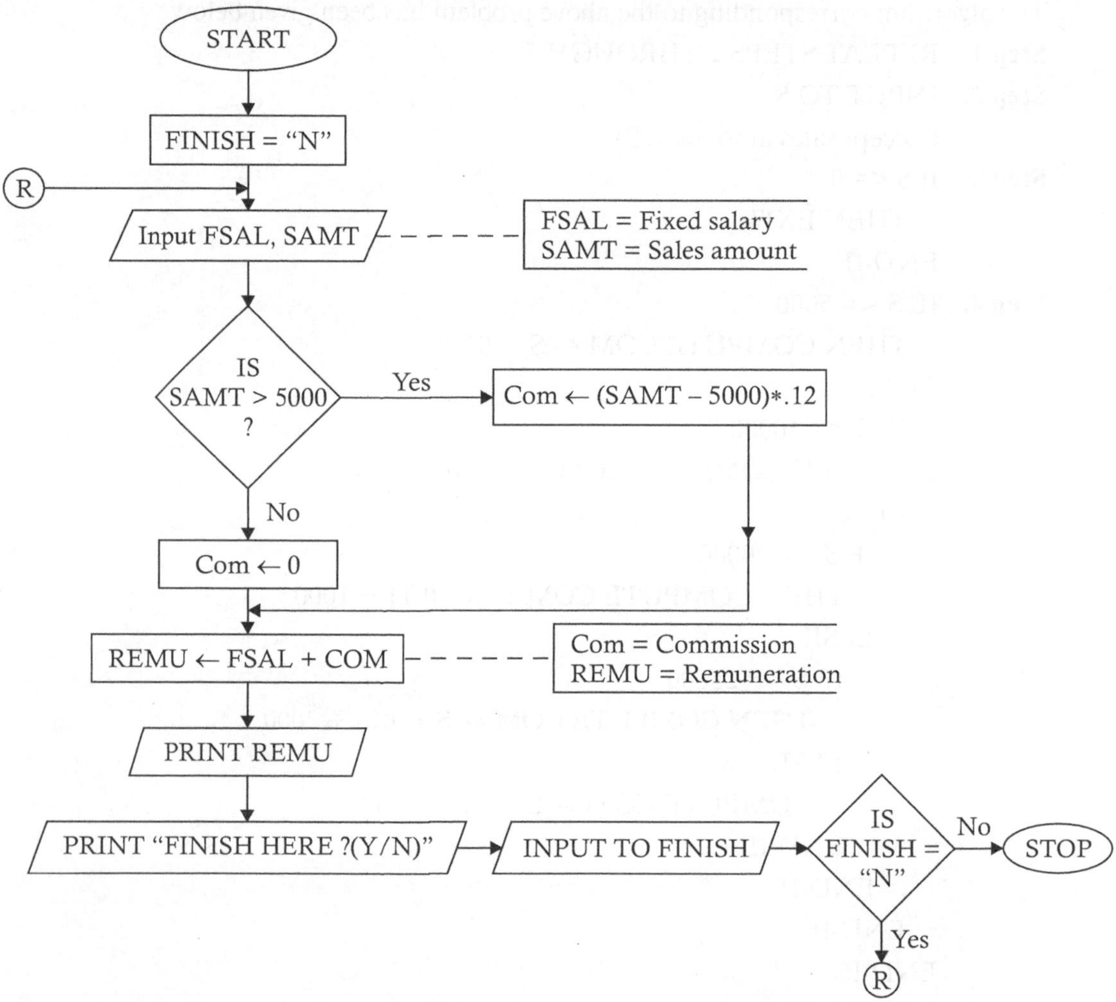

The algorithm corresponding to the above problem is given below :

Step 1. FINISH ← "N"

Step 2. REPEAT STEPS 3 THROUGH 9 WHILE FINISH = "N"

Step 3. INPUT TO FSAL, SAMT

Step 4. IF SAMT > 5000

THEN COMPUTE COM ← (SAMT – 5000) * .12

ELSE

COM ← 0

END-IF

Step 5. COMPUTE REMU ← FSAL + COM

Step 6. PRINT "REMUNERATION IS", REMU

Step 7. PRINT "FINISH (Y/N) ?"

Step 8. INPUT TO FINISH
Step 9. IF FINISH = "Y"
THEN EXIT
END-IF
Step 10. STOP

Problem 3.3. *A labour contractor pays the workers at the end of each week according to the rules given below :*

For the first 35 hours of work, the rate of pay is Rs. 15 per hour ; for the next 25 hours, the rate of pay is Rs. 18 per hour ; for the rest, if any, the rate of pay is Rs. 26 per hour. No worker is allowed to work for more than 80 hours in a week. Develop a flowchart to show how wage of the workers can be calculated on the basis of valid inputs.

Task Analysis. It is clear from the given rules that the input required is total hours worked. The rates of payment depend on different slabs of the hours worked and are given. The total hours worked may be considered valid if it lies in the range of 0 through 80. So, our procedure for evaluating the wage will consists of (*i*) validation of hours worked given, (*ii*) checking the slab to which the hours worked pertain and then (*iii*) application of different rates to calculate the wage. The procedure is shown within a loop and it is terminated when zero or some negative value is given as input against hours worked. The following flowchart illustrates the procedure.

The algorithm corresponding to the above problem has been given below :

```
Step 1. REPEAT STEPS 2 THROUGH 6
Step 2. INPUT TO TH
Step 3. IF TH <= 0
          THEN EXIT
        END-IF
Step 4. IF TH > 80
          THEN PRINT "INVALID HOURS"
          CONTINUE
        END-IF
Step 5. IF TH <= 35
          THEN COMPUTE WAGE ← TH*15
        ELSE
          IF TH <= 60
            THEN COMPUTE WAGE ← 35*15 + (TH–35)*18
          ELSE
            COMPUTE WAGE ← 35*15 + 25*18 + (TH–60)*25
          END-IF
        END-IF
Step 6. PRINT "WAGE IS", WAGE
Step 7. STOP
```

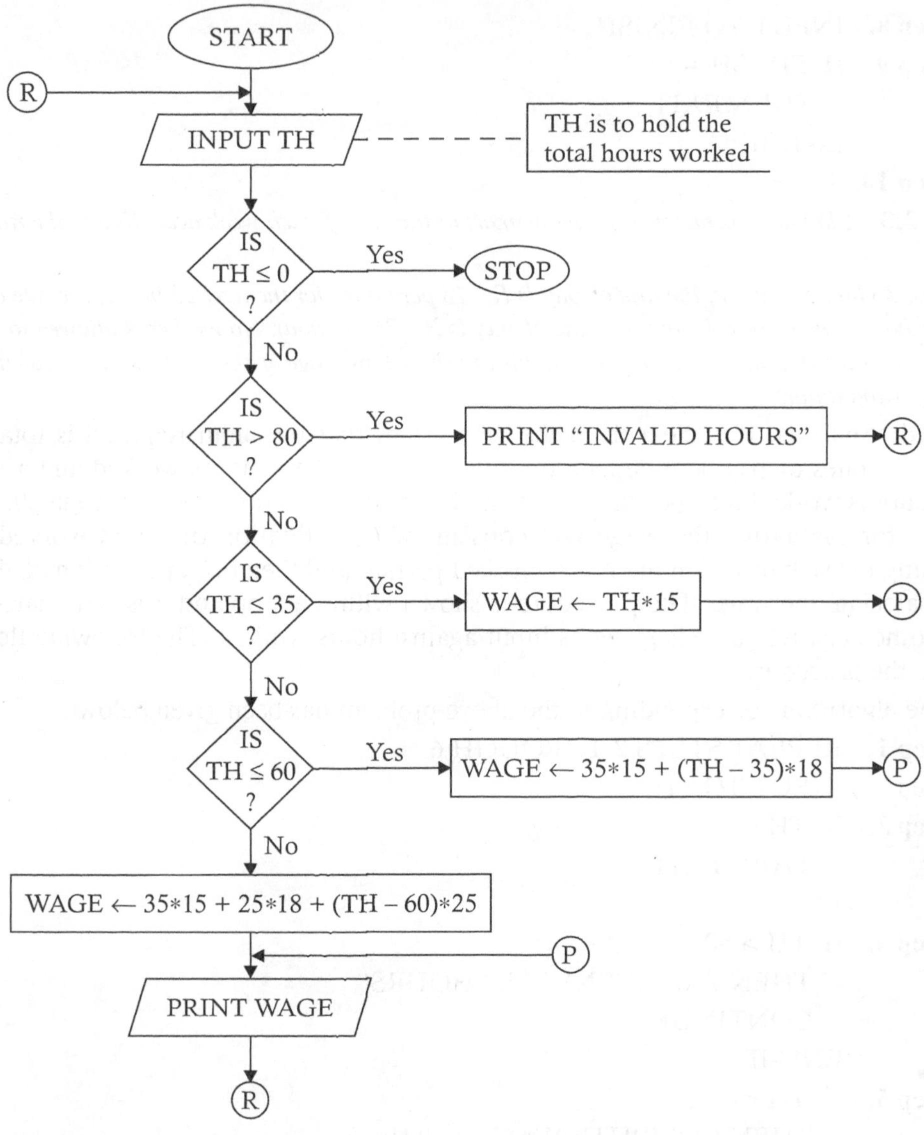

Problem 3.4. *In a certain city the telephone bill is calculated according to the following rules for the first 300 calls, the bill is fixed and it is equal to Rs. 500 ; for the next 65 calls, the rate per call is Re. 0.95 ; for the next 90 calls, the rate per call is Rs. 1.50 ; for calls beyond that the rate per call is Rs. 2.25 per call. Develop a flowchart to show how the telephone bill is calculated.*

Task Analysis. Here we observe that the input required is the number of calls and the output required is the total bill for the telephone calls. Note that the rates vary at different slabs only for the excess number of calls in the particular slab. The following flowchart demonstrates the formulas for calculating the bill at different slabs.

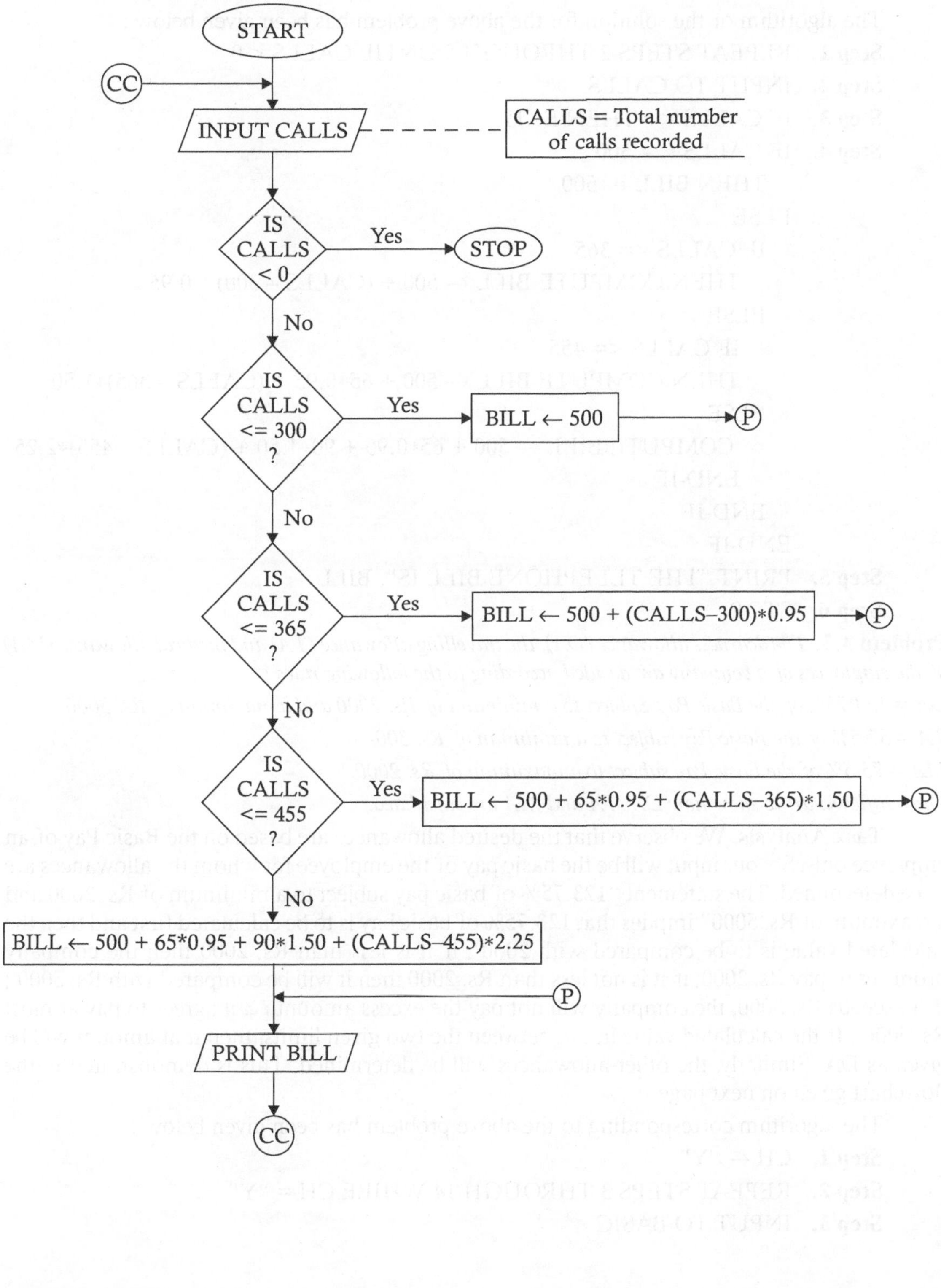
START
CC
INPUT CALLS
CALLS = Total number of calls recorded
IS CALLS < 0
Yes
STOP
No
IS CALLS <= 300 ?
Yes
BILL ← 500
P
No
IS CALLS <= 365 ?
Yes
BILL ← 500 + (CALLS–300)*0.95
P
No
IS CALLS <= 455 ?
Yes
BILL ← 500 + 65*0.95 + (CALLS–365)*1.50
P
No
BILL ← 500 + 65*0.95 + 90*1.50 + (CALLS–455)*2.25
P
PRINT BILL
CC

The algorithm of the solution for the above problem has been given below :

Step 1. REPEAT STEPS 2 THROUGH 5 UNTIL CALLS < 0

Step 2. INPUT TO CALLS

Step 3. IF CALLS < 0 THEN EXIT

Step 4. IF CALLS < = 300

```
   THEN BILL ← 500
ELSE
   IF CALLS <= 365
      THEN COMPUTE BILL ← 500 + (CALLS – 300) * 0.95
   ELSE
      IF CALLS <= 455
      THEN COMPUTE BILL ← 500 + 65*0.95 + (CALLS – 365)*1.50
   ELSE
       COMPUTE BILL ← 500 + 65*0.95 + 90*1.50 + (CALLS – 455)*2.25
      END-IF
   END-IF
END-IF
```

Step 5. PRINT "THE TELEPHONE BILL IS", BILL

Step 6. STOP

Problem 3.5. *The dearness allowance (DA), the travelling allowance (TA) and medical allowance (MA) of the employees of a company are decided according to the following rules :*

DA = 123.75% of the Basic Pay Subject to a minimum of Rs. 2000 and a maximum of Rs. 5000.

TA = 57.5% of the Basic Pay subject to a minimum of Rs. 300.

MA = 73.5% of the Basic Pay subject to a maximum of Rs. 2000.

Draw a flowchart to show how DA, TA and MA are calculated.

Task Analysis. We observe that the desired allowances are based on the Basic Pay of an employee only. So, our input will be the basic pay of the employee for whom the allowances are to be determined. The statement "123.75% of basic pay subject to a minimum of Rs. 2000 and a maximum of Rs. 5000" implies that 123.75% of basic bay is to be calculated first and then the calculated value is to be compared with 2000 ; if it is less than Rs. 2000 then the company promises to pay Rs. 2000; if it is not less than Rs. 2000 then it will be compared with Rs. 5000 ; if it exceeds Rs. 5000, the company will not pay the excess amount *i.e.* it agrees to pay at most Rs. 5000 : If the calculated value lies in between the two given limits, then that amount will be given as DA. Similarly, the other allowances will be determined. This is demonstrated in the flowchart given on next page.

The algorithm corresponding to the above problem has been given below :

Step 1. CH ← "Y"

Step 2. REPEAT STEPS 3 THROUGH 14 WHILE CH = "Y"

Step 3. INPUT TO BASIC

Step 4. COMPUTE DA ← BASIC∗123.75/100
Step 5. IF DA < 2000
THEN DA ← 2000
ELSE
IF DA > 5000
THEN DA ← 5000
END-IF
END-IF

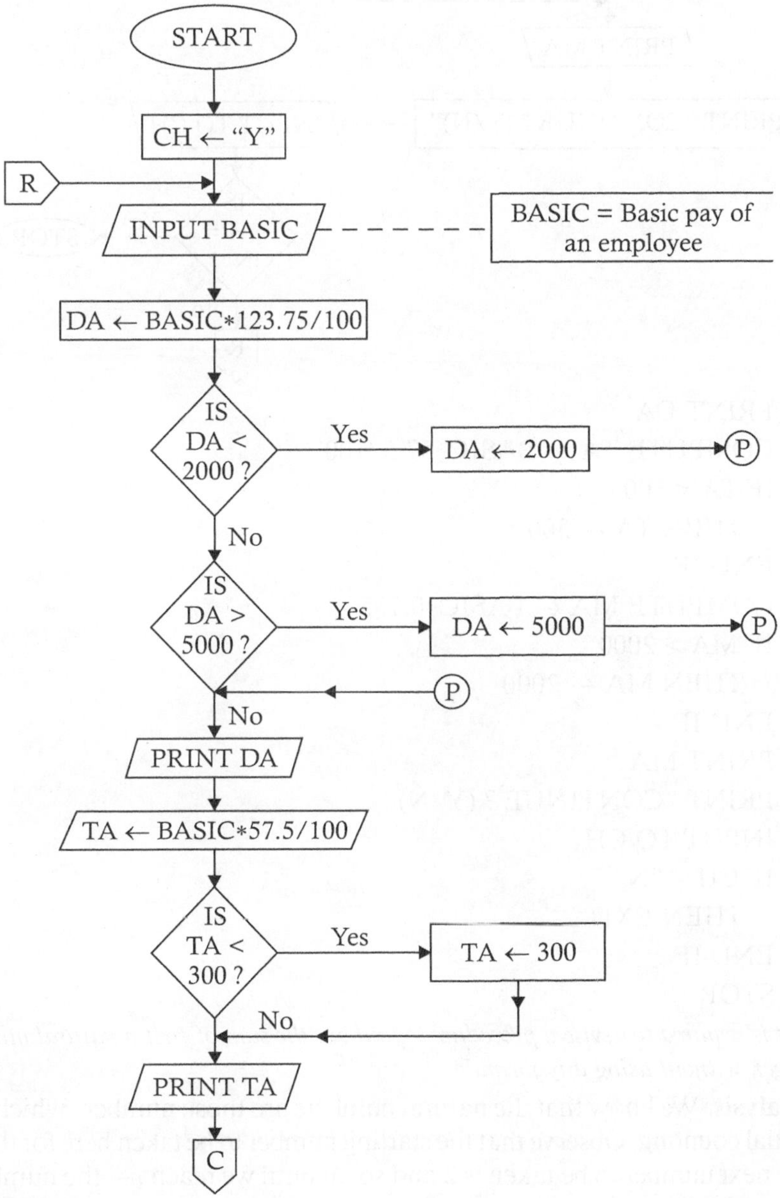

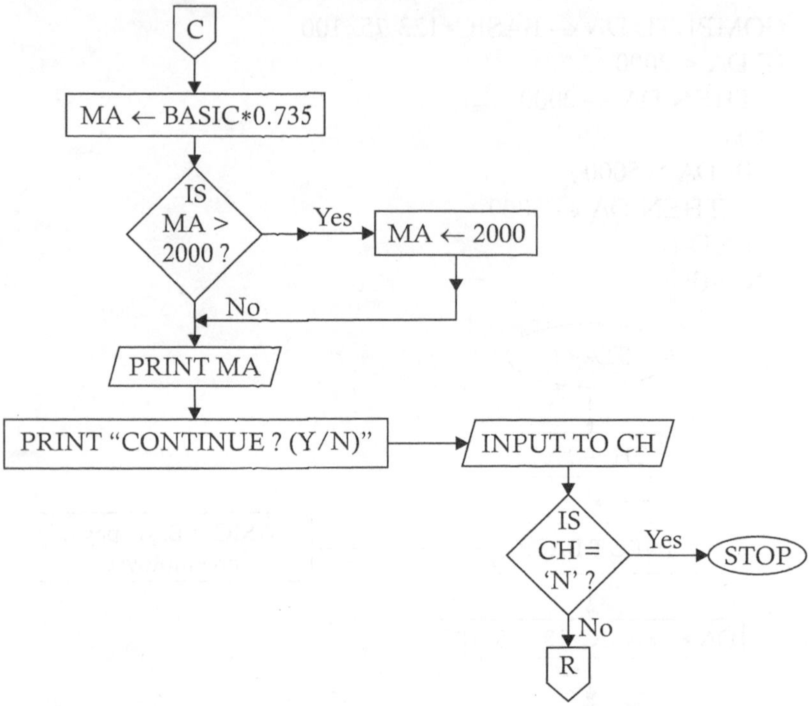

Step 6. PRINT DA
Step 7. COMPUTE TA ← BASIC*57.5/100
Step 8. IF TA < 300
    THEN TA ← 300
  END-IF
Step 9. COMPUTE MA ← BASIC*0.735
Step 10. IF MA > 2000
    THEN MA ← 2000
  END-IF
Step 11. PRINT MA
Step 12. PRINT "CONTINUE ? (Y/N)"
Step 13. INPUT TO CH
Step 14. IF CH = "N"
    THEN EXIT
  END-IF
Step 15. STOP

Problem 3.6. *It is required to devise a procedure to find out the sum of first n natural numbers, where n is any given integer, without using any formula.*

Task Analysis. We know that the natural numbers are those numbers which are obtained through sequential counting. Observe that the starting number to be taken here for the summation process is 1, the next number to be taken is 2 and so on until we reach *n*—the number of natural numbers to be summed. The numbers to be added up are known as inputs and can be generated by instructing the computer. So we assign the value 1 to a variable to simulate the first natural number. We then add the value of the variable to some accumulator. The accumulator must then contain some initial value to make the summation process semantically correct *i.e.* meaningful. This initial value must be 0 in this case because we are adding the first number. We can then increase the value of the variable containing the first natural number by 1. This next number which is 2 in this case can then be added to the current value of the accumulator to obtain the sum of first two natural numbers. In this way we can continue the generation and summation process until we add up all the natural numbers including N for some given value of N. But we must also keep a count of the numbers that are being added ; otherwise we will not be able to decide whether we have added the desired N numbers or not. So a variable is to be used here as a counter. This counter must be initialised to zero first from which we can increment its value each time by 1 when we add some number to the value of the accumulator. This procedure is illustrated in the flowchart below :

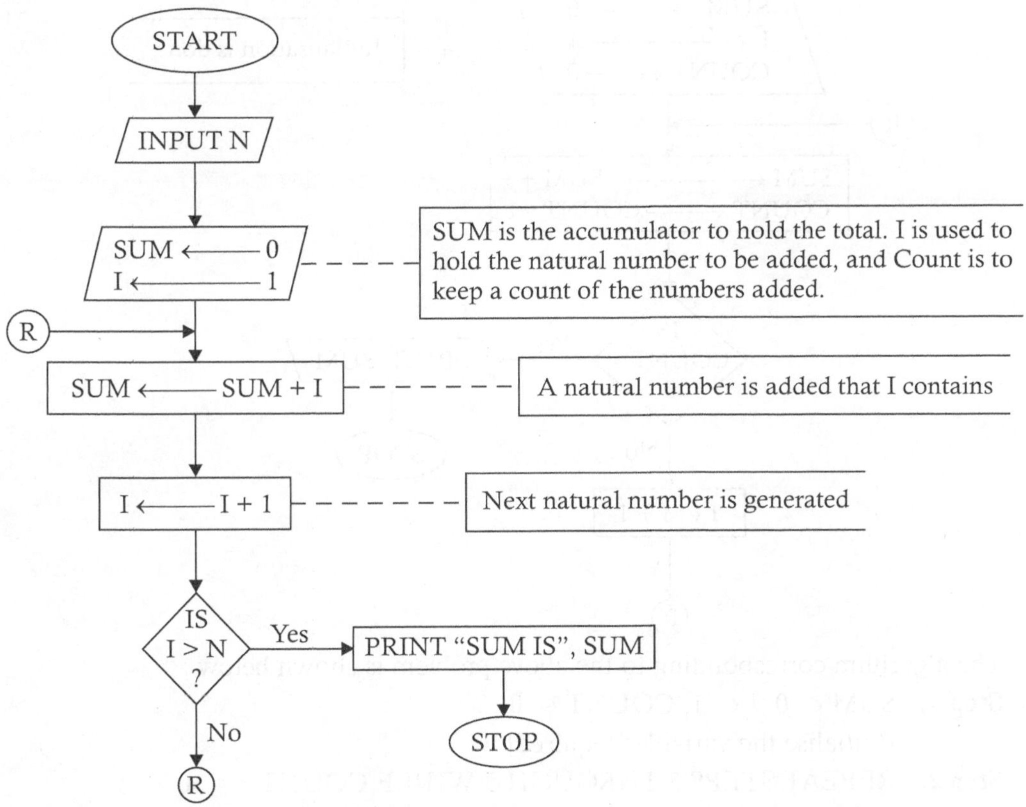

The algorithm corresponding to the above flowchart has been stated below :

Step 1. INPUT "ENTER NO. OF TERMS TO ADD" TO N

Step 2. SUM ← 0 [INITIALISATION]

Step 3. I ← 1 [INITIALISATION]

Step 4. REPEAT STEPS 5 THROUGH 6 WHILE I <= N.
Step 5. COMPUTE SUM ← SUM + I
Step 6. COMPUTE I ← I + 1
Step 7. PRINT "THE SUM IS", SUM
Step 8. STOP

Problem 3.7. *Draw a flowchart to show how to obtain the sum of first 30 natural numbers.*

Task Analysis. This problem is similar to problem 3.6. The only difference is that the number of natural numbers to be added up is given as a constant (30). So we need not ask for any input from the user.

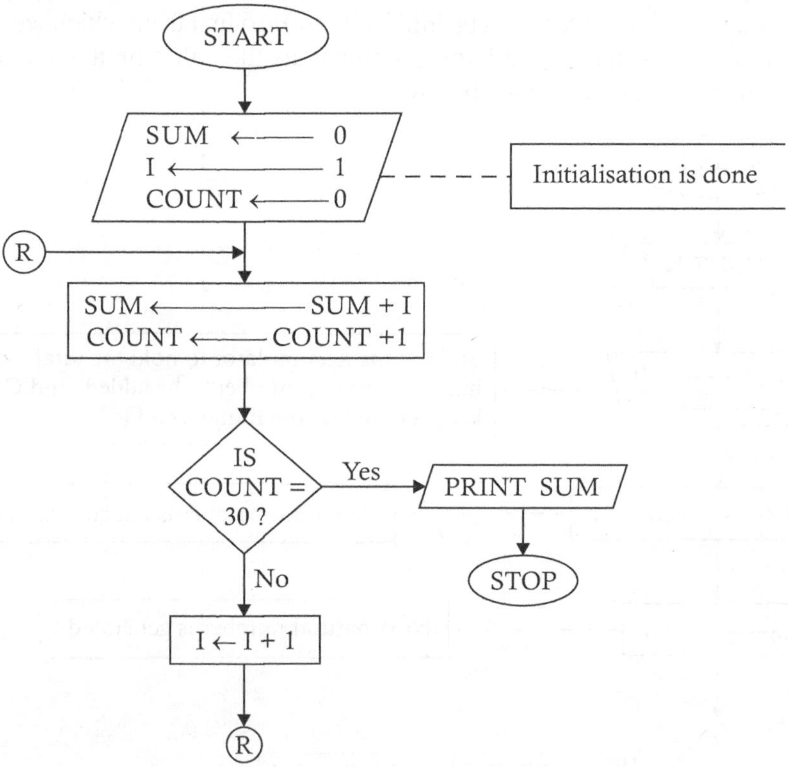

The algorithm corresponding to the above problem is shown below :

Step 1. SUM ← 0, I ← 1, COUNT ← 0
[Initialise the variables required]
Step 2. REPEAT STEPS 3 THROUGH 5 WHILE COUNT <= 30
Step 3. COMPUTE SUM ← SUM + I
Step 4. COMPUTE COUNT ← COUNT + 1
Step 5. COMPUTE I ← I + 1
Step 6. PRINT "THE SUM IS", SUM
Step 7. STOP

Problem 3.8. *Draw a flowchart to show how to find the product of first 10 natural numbers.*

Task Analysis. Here we require the product of the first 10 natural numbers. The natural numbers are defined in the task analysis of problem 3.6. So the natural numbers can be generated similarly. To hold the product, we require a location that is initialised with 1 so that we can specify how to obtain the new product by multiplying the current product by the natural number currently in use because only the initial value 1 will keep the content of the location for product unchanged when the value of the product location is multiplied by 1. This is illustrated below :

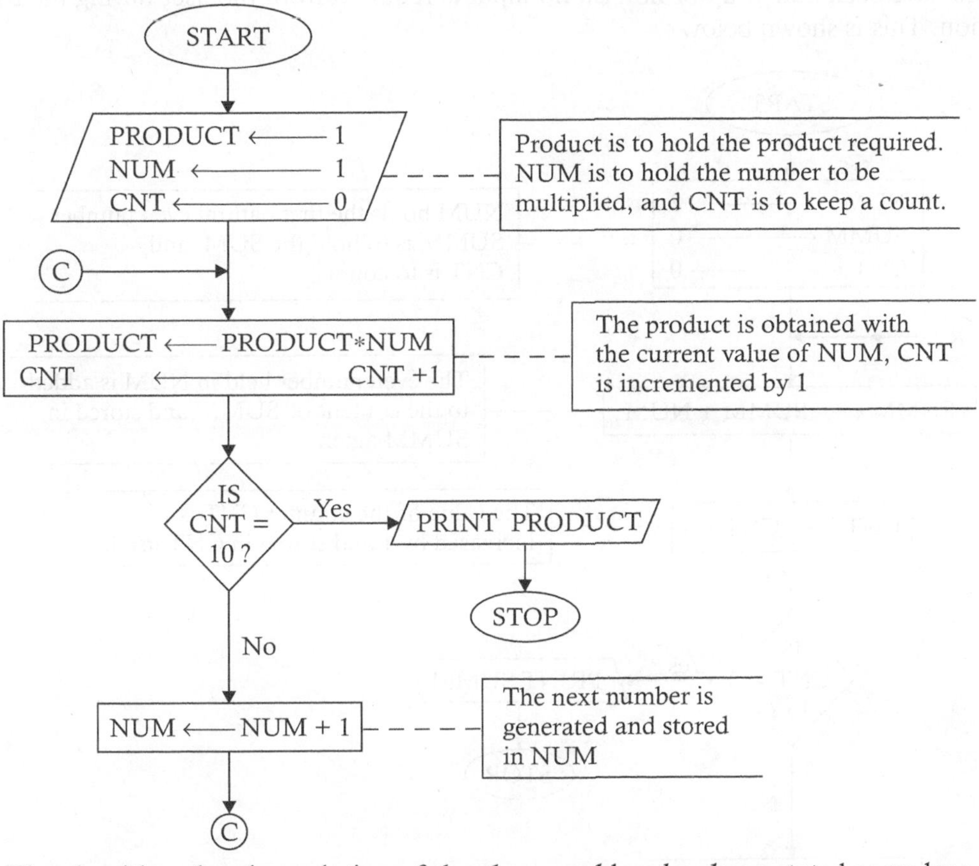

The algorithm showing solution of the above problem has been stated as under :

Step 1. PRODUCT ← 1, NUM ← 1, CNT ← 0
(Initialise variables required)

Step 2. REPEAT STEPS 3 THROUGH 5 WHILE CNT <= 10

Step 3. COMPUTE PRODUCT ← PRODUCT*NUM

Step 4. COMPUTE CNT ← CNT + 1
(Increment the Counter)

Step 5. COMPUTE NUM ← NUM + 1 (The next number is generated)

Step 6. PRINT "THE PRODUCT IS", PRODUCT

Step 7. STOP

Problem 3.9. *Draw a flowchart to find the sum of first 15 even natural numbers.*

Task Analysis. We know that the first natural even number is 2 and the next natural even number *i.e.*, the second even number can be obtained by adding 2 to the first natural number. The successive natural even numbers can be obtained by adding 2 to the preceding natural even number. These even numbers can be accumulated in a location by adding the generated even number each time to the accumulator which will contain zero initially.

A count of the numbers added will enable us to check whether first 15 even natural numbers have been added up or not. So no input is required from the user during the time of execution. This is shown below :

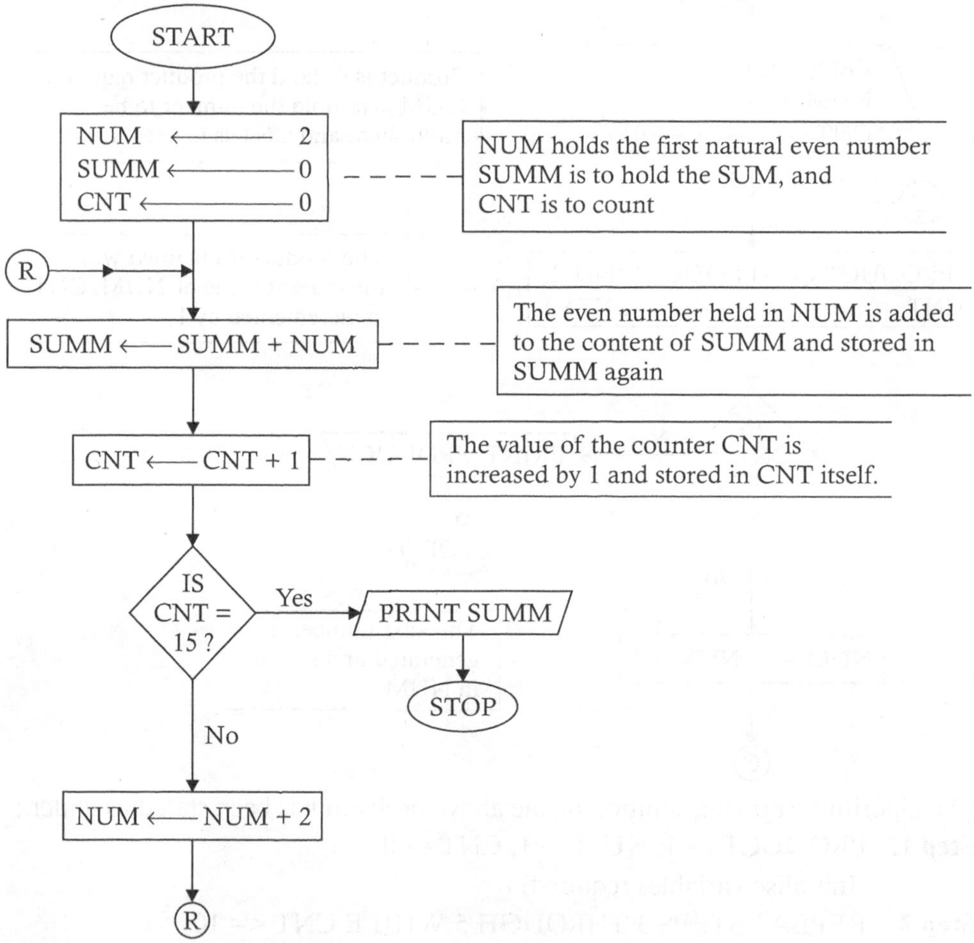

The algorithm showing the solution of the above problem is as given below :

Step 1. [Initialise the accumulator, counter and variable]
SUMM ← 0, CNT ← 0, NUM ← 2

Step 2. REPEAT STEPS 3 THROUGH 5 WHILE CNT < 15

Step 3. COMPUTE SUMM ← SUMM + NUM

Step 4. COMPUTE CNT ← CNT + 1

Step 5. COMPUTE NUM ← NUM + 2

Step 6. PRINT "THE DESIRED SUM IS", SUMM

Step 7. STOP

Problem 3.10. *Construct a flowchart to show how consecutive even numbers starting from 2 are summed up until the sum just exceeds 1000 and then to show the sum and the number of even numbers added.*

Task Analysis. Here the starting input is given as the first even number and we are required to sum up the consecutive even numbers. These even numbers can be generated by adding 2 each time to the preceding even number as shown earlier. The terminating condition is not a count but the total of the even numbers being summed up when the total just exceeds 1000. A count of the numbers added to make the sum exceeding 1000 is also required in the output. So we need to maintain a counter also. As the input data values can be generated through a procedure easily, we need not accept any input from the terminal during the time of execution. This is illustrated below :

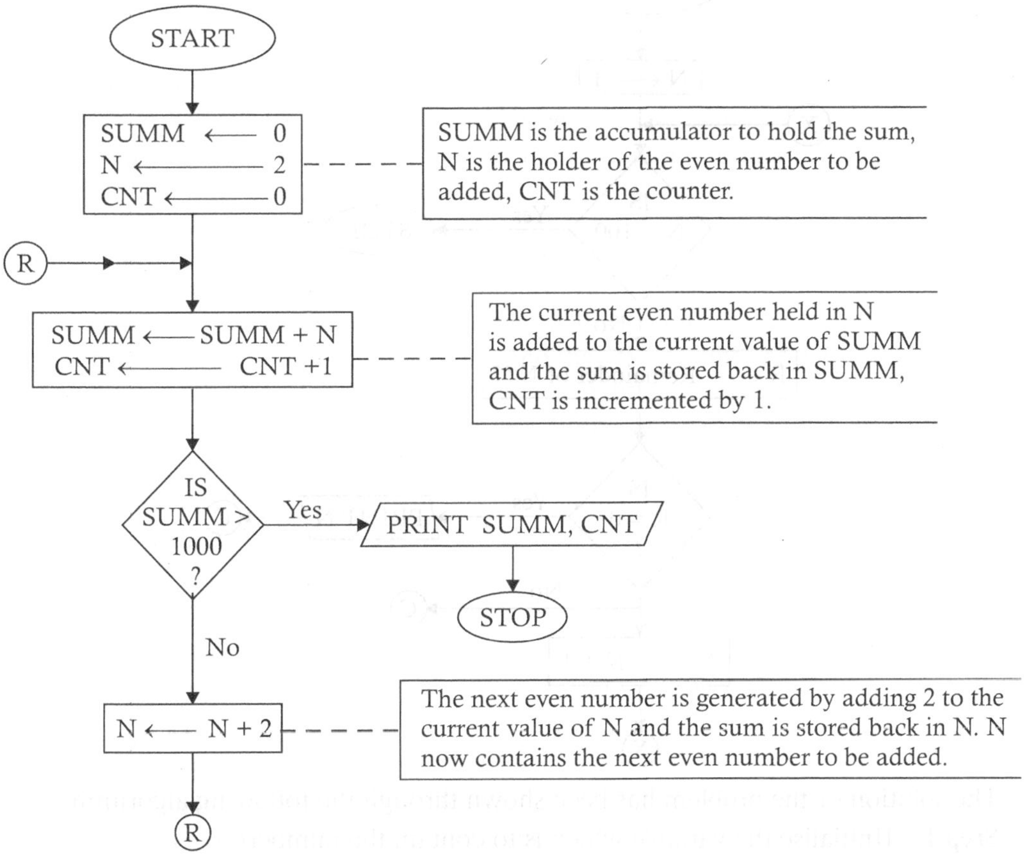

The solution of the given problem has been shown through following algorithm :

Step 1. [Initialise the required variables]

SUMM ← 0, N ← 2, CNT ← 0

Step 6. IF MNO <= 3
    THEN COMPUTE CHG ← ND*1.75
  ELSE
    IF MNO <= 6
      THEN COMPUTE CHG ← ND*1.65

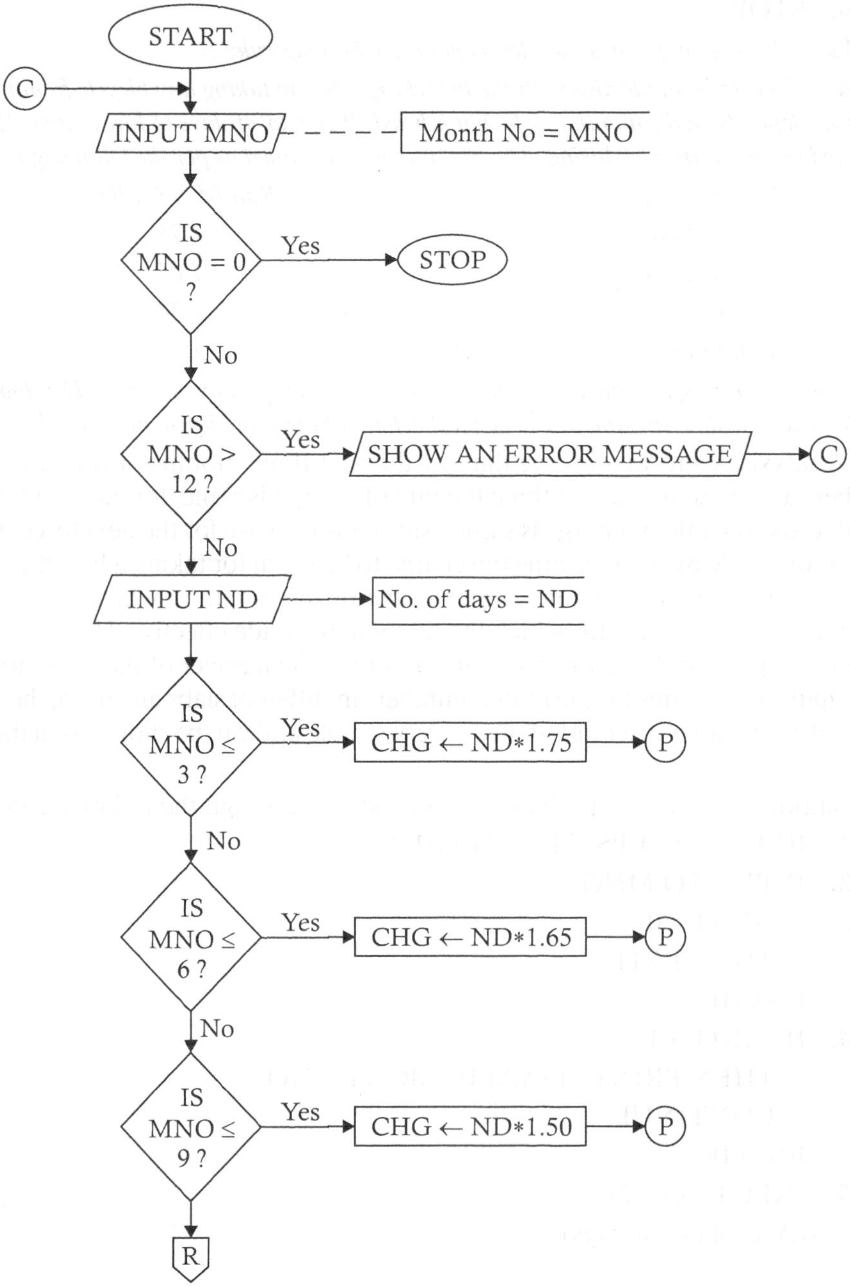

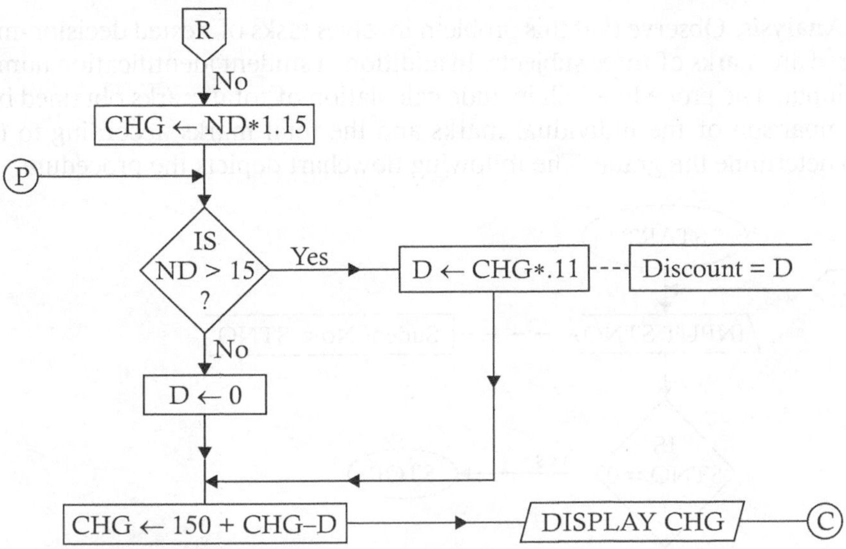


```
ELSE
   IF MNO <= 9
      THEN COMPUTE CHG ← ND*1.50
   ELSE
      COMPUTE CHG ← ND*1.15
   END-IF
 END-IF
END-IF
```

Step 7. IF ND > 15

```
   THEN COMPUTE D ← CHG*.11
ELSE
   D ← 0
END-IF
```

Step 8. COMPUTE CHG ← 150 + CHG – D

Step 9. DISPLAY "THE CHARGE OF HIRING", CHG

Step 10. STOP

Problem 3.13. *Draw a flowchart for the following problem to determine the grade. In an institute 3 tests on three different subjects are held. On the basis of marks in the three subjects say M1, M2 and M3, a grade is awarded to each student as per the following rules :*

(a) If the score in each subject be more than 80, and the total is more than 250, the grade is A +

(b) If the score in each subject be more than 60, and the total is more than 200, the grade is A

(c) If the score in any one or more subjects be less than 50, the grade is F

(d) In all other cases the grade is B.

Task Analysis. Observe that this problem involves tasks of nested decision-making. The inputs required are marks of three subjects. In addition, a student identification number may be accepted as input. The procedure will include calculation of total marks obtained by a student and then comparison of the individual marks and the total marks according to the rules of gradation to determine the grade. The following flowchart depicts the procedure.

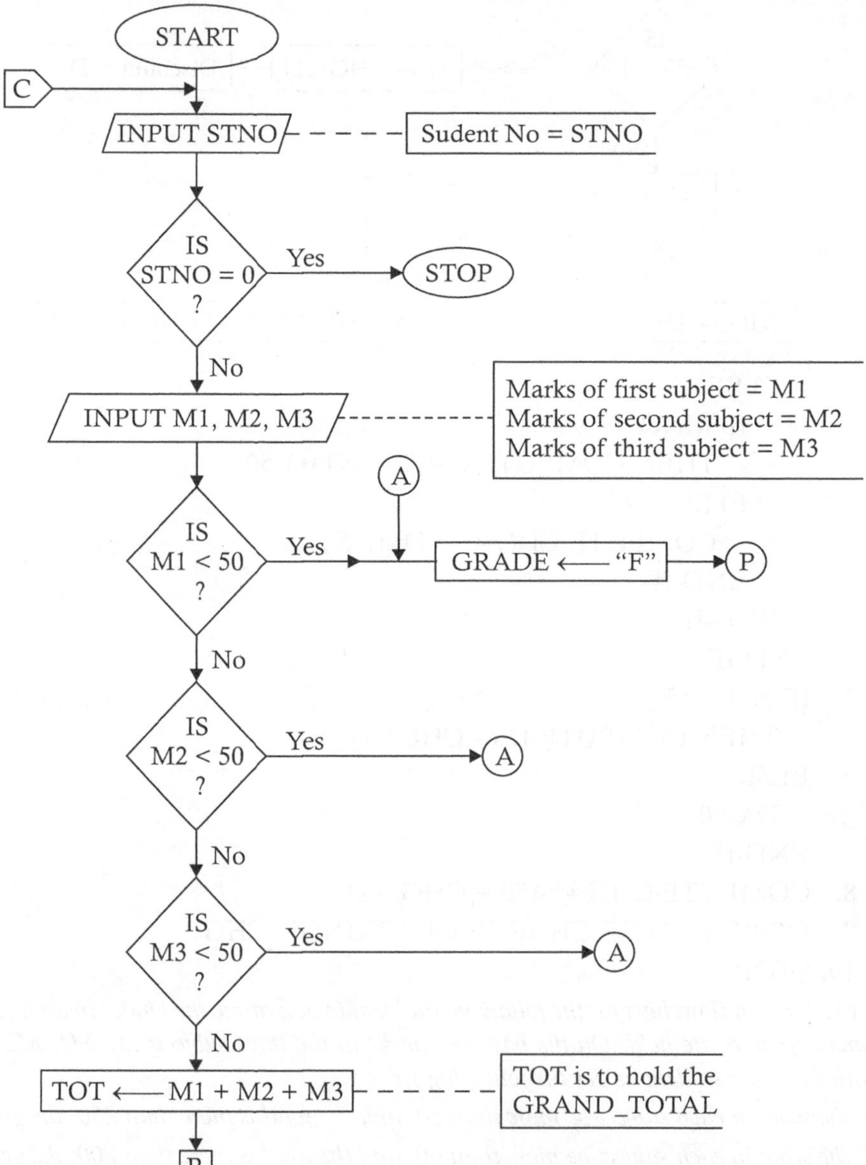

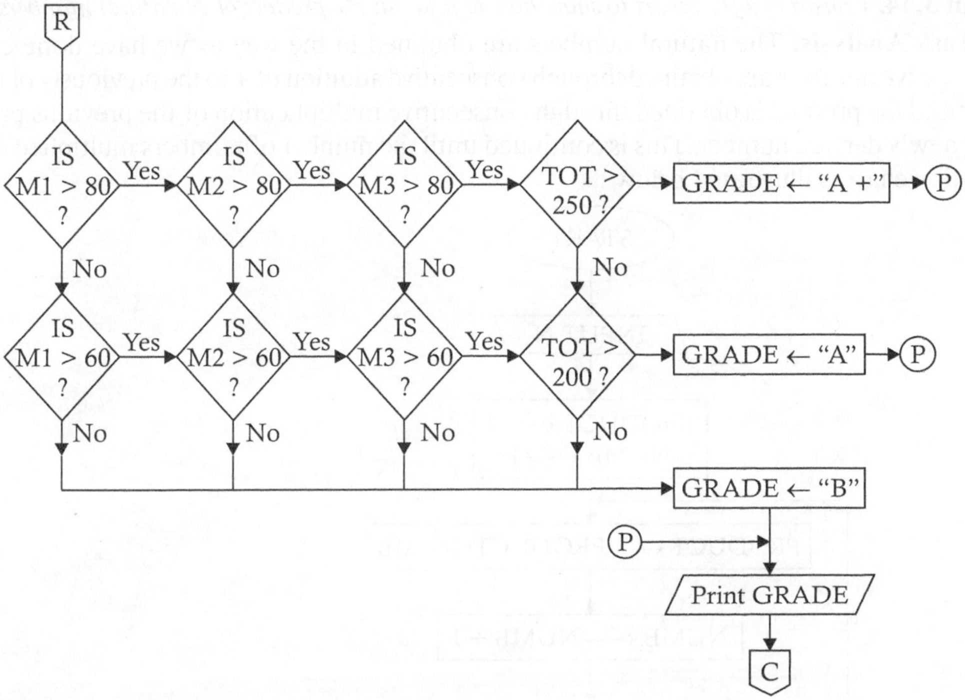

The solution of the problem above has been stated through the following algorithm :

Step 1. FOR EACH STNO DO

Step 2. INPUT TO STNO

Step 3. IF STNO = 0 THEN EXIT
END-IF

Step 4. INPUT TO M1, M2, M3

Step 5. IF M1 < 50 OR M2 < 50 OR M3 < 50
THEN GRADE ← "F"
END-IF

Step 6. COMPUTE TOT ← M1 + M2 + M3

Step 7. IF M1 > 80 AND M2 > 80 AND M3 > 80 AND TOT > 250
THEN GRADE ← "A+"
ELSE IF M1 > 60 AND M2 > 60 AND M3 > 60 AND TOT > 200
THEN GRADE ← "A"
ELSE
GRADE ← "B"
END-IF
END-IF

Step 8. PRINT GRADE

Step 9. END-FOR

Step 10. STOP

Problem 3.14. *Construct a flowchart to show how to find out the product of N natural numbers.*

Task Analysis. The natural numbers are obtained in the way as we have done earlier. The successive numbers are obtained through consecutive addition of 1 to the previously obtained number and the product is obtained through consecutive multiplication of the previous product and the newly derived number. This is continued until the number of numbers multiplied equals N. The flowchart is illustrated below :

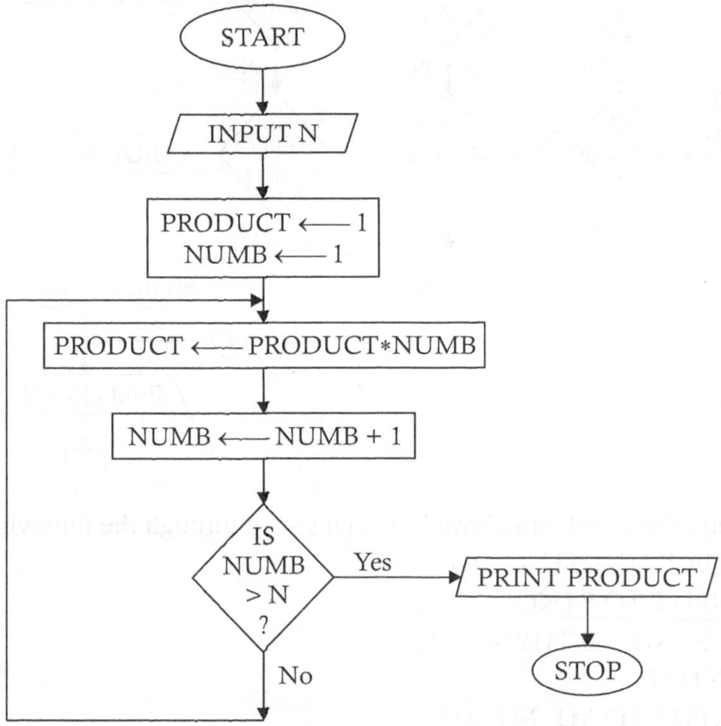

The algorithm showing solution of the above problem has been given below :

Step 1. INPUT TO N

Step 2. [INITIALISE VARIABLES REQUIRED]
PRODUCT ← 1, NUMB ← 1

Step 3. REPEAT WHILE NUMB <= N

Step 4. COMPUTE PRODUCT ← PRODUCT*NUMB
[CALCULATE PRODUCT]

Step 5. COMPUTE NUMB ← NUMB + 1
[INCREMENT NUMB]

Step 6. END-WHILE

Step 7. PRINT PRODUCT

Step 8. STOP

Problem 3.15. *Draw a flowchart to show how to find out all even natural numbers which are divisible by 7 between a given range.*

Task Analysis. Here we require two numbers which will serve as boundary values between all the desired numbers to be generated. If a number within the given range is found to be divisible by 7 then it is to be printed. As the range may include a large number of numbers, each of the numbers need not be accepted as input from the terminal because it will slow down the whole process. So on the basis of the lower range given we shall generate natural numbers one by one and then we shall test the divisibility by 7. A number is said to be divisible by 7, if it leaves a zero remainder when divided by 7. So the input will be the numbers forming the lower and the upper range between which we shall test all the numbers including the numbers forming the ranges. A loop is required to perform the same task of divisibility checking with a newly generated number. The following flowchart depicts procedure.

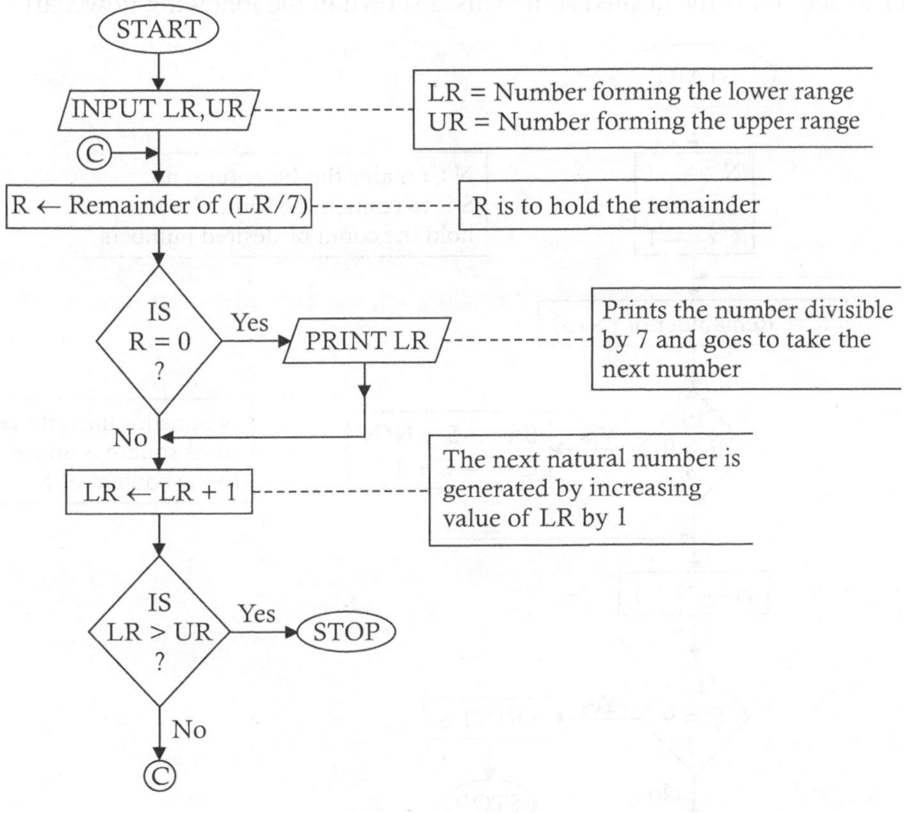

The solution of the above problem has been shown through the following algorithm :

Step 1. INPUT TO LR, UR

Step 2. REPEAT STEPS 3 THROUGH 5 UNTIL LR > UR

Step 3. COMPUTE R ← REMAINDER OF (LR/7)

Step 4. IF R = 0 THEN PRINT LR END-IF

Step 5. COMPUTE LR ← LR + 1
(INCREASE THE VALUE OF LR)

Step 6. STOP

Problem 3.16. *Construct a flowchart to find out the sum of the squares of first 9 natural numbers which are divisible by 3.*

Task Analysis. Observe that the problem demands the natural numbers divisible by 3 to obtain their square values and then to accumulate 9 such consecutive square values as the sum of the values.

So our procedure to obtain the sum will encompass generating natural numbers one by one, testing each for divisibility by 3 and if one is found to be divisible, obtaining the square of the number to determine the desired sum. This is shown in the following flowchart :

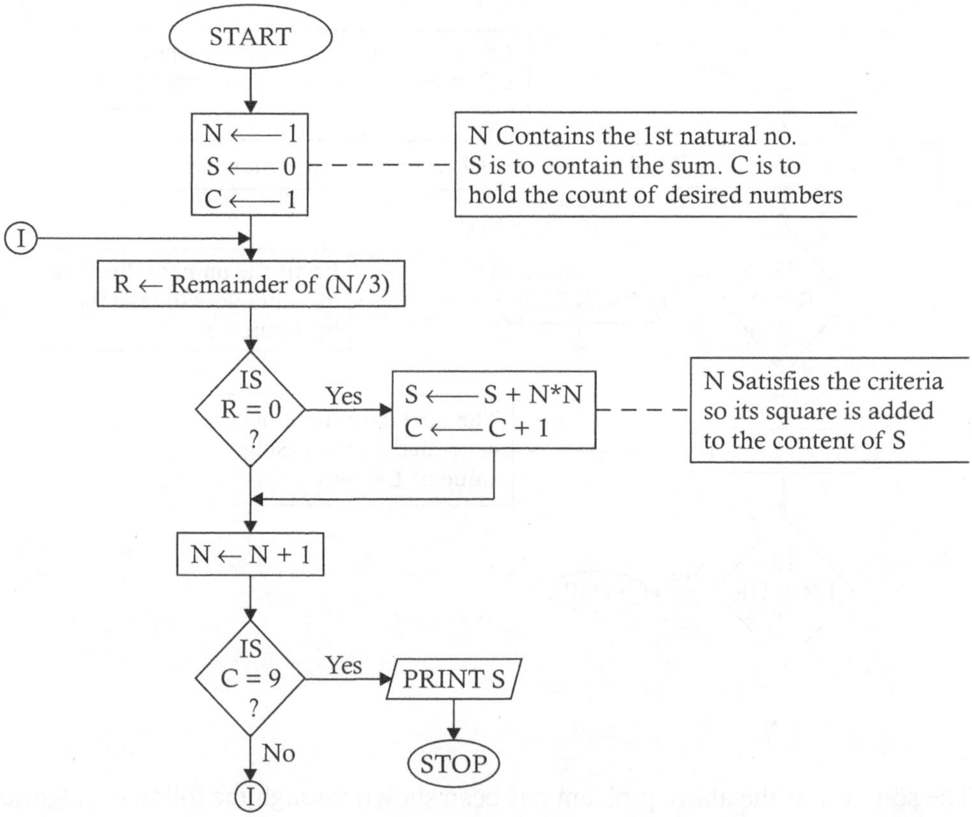

The solution of the above problem has been shown through the following algorithm :

Step 1. [INITIALISE VARIABLES]
N ← 1
S ← 1
C ← 1

Step 2. REPEAT WHILE C <= 9

Step 3. COMPUTE R ← REMAINDER OF (N/3)

Step 4. IF R = 0

THEN COMPUTE S ← S + N*N

COMPUTE C ← C + 1

END-IF

Step 5. COMPUTE N ← N + 1

Step 6. PRINT S

Step 7. STOP

Problem 3.17. *Construct a flowchart to show how to find the sum of all the numbers which are divisible by P but not divisible by Q within a given range.*

Task Analysis. Note that we are required to test the natural numbers one by one which fall within a given range and are divisible by some given number *p* but not divisible by another given number Q. So we require four inputs from the user of this procedure, namely, lower and upper ranges of the numbers to be checked, P and Q. The natural numbers can be generated serially as done earlier. We have also seen how the divisibility can be checked. So the procedure can be shown as under.

The algorithm of the solution for the above problem has been shown below :

Step 1. INPUT TO LR, UR, P, Q

Step 2. [INITIALISE] N ← LR, S ← 0

Step 3. REPEAT STEPS 4 TO 6 UNTIL N > UR

Step 4. COMPUTE R1 ← N% P

COMPUTE R2 ← N% Q

Step 5. IF R1 = 0 AND R2 NOT = 0

THEN COMPUTE S ← S + N

END-IF

Step 6. COMPUTE N ← N + 1

Step 7. PRINT S

Step 8. STOP

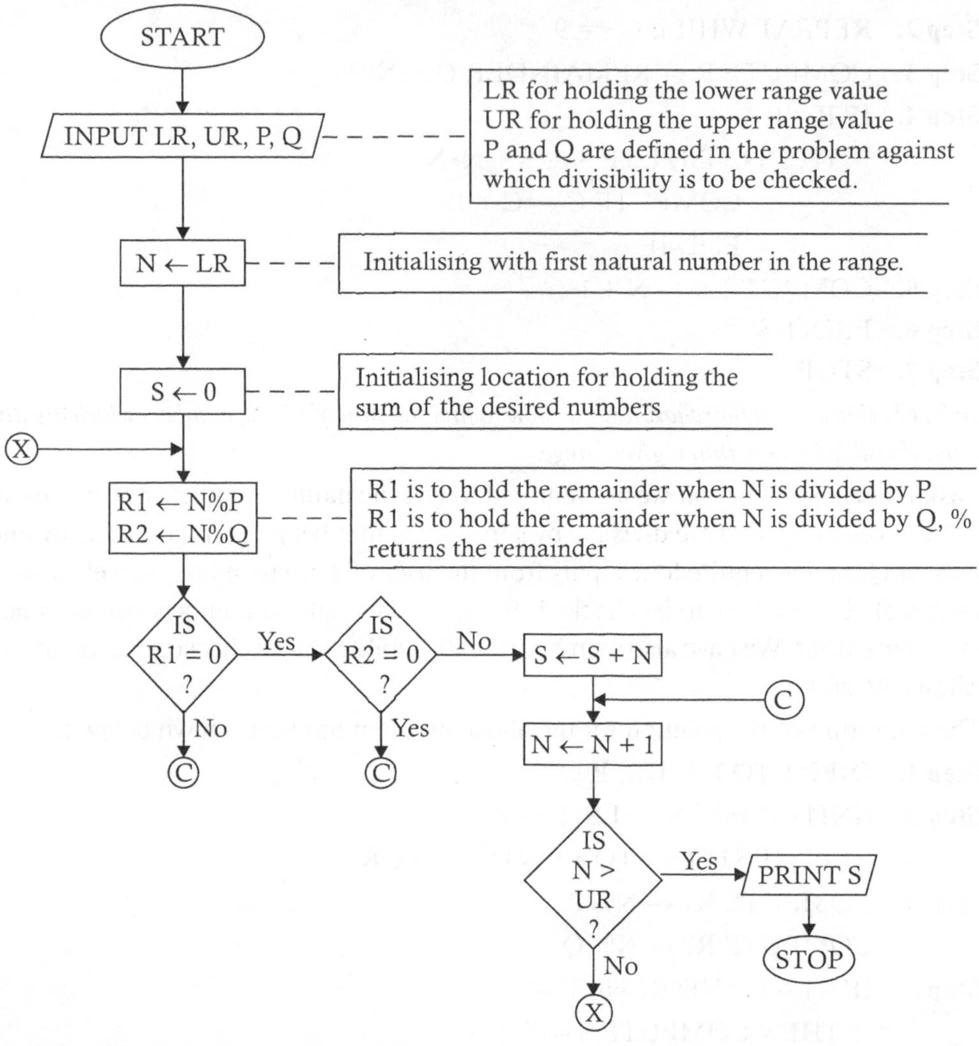

Problem 3.18. *Draw a flowchart to show how to obtain the HCF and LCM of two given numbers :*

Task Analysis. We know that HCF (Highest Common Factor) of two numbers is the largest number that can divide the two numbers without leaving any remainder and the LCM (Lowest common multiple) of two numbers is the smaller number which is divisible by both the numbers. The best way to obtain the HCF is the method of division in which one number is divided by another number to see if the remainder is zero, then the divisor number is the HCF, if it is other than zero then the divisor is made the dividend, the remainder is made the divisor and the division is repeated to obtain the remainder again. This change of dividend and divisor is done repeatedly until we get the divisor that leaves zero as remainder and the divisor in the last case will be the HCF of the given numbers.

To find out the LCM, the easiest way is to use the relationship between HCF and LCM. We know that the product of two numbers equals the product of their HCF and LCM. So the LCM can be obtained easily by dividing the product of the given numbers by that HCF. This formula can be described alternatively as under.

LCM × HCF of two numbers = Product of the two numbers

$$\textbf{LCM of two numbers} = \frac{\textbf{Product of the two numbers}}{\textbf{HCF of the two numbers}}$$

So to solve the given problem we require two inputs only, namely, the two numbers for which we require to determine the HCF and LCM. The procedure described above is depicted in the following flowchart :

The following flowchart is for obtaining the HCF and LCM of two given numbers :

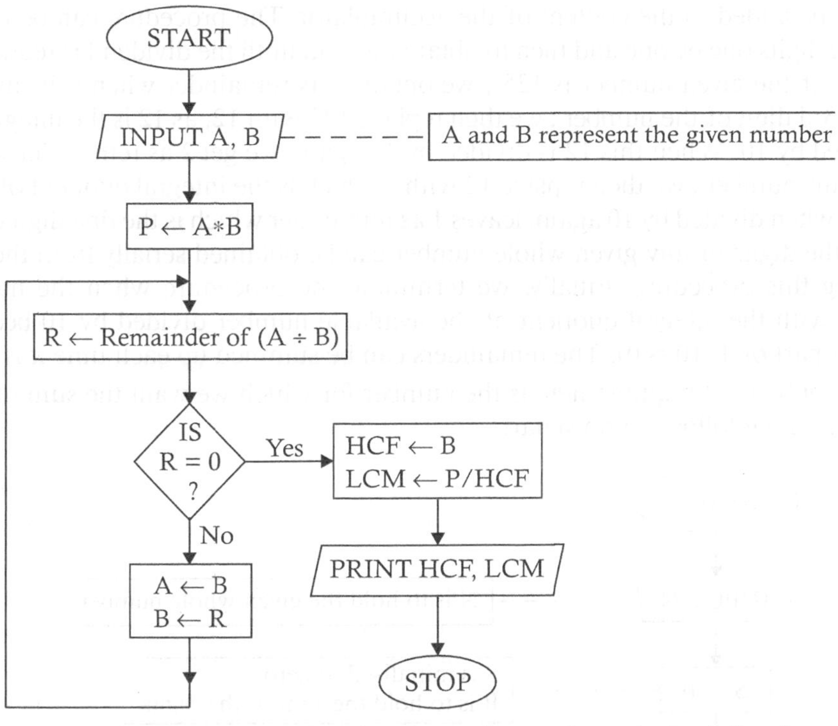

The solution of the above problem has been shown through the following algorithm :

Step 1. INPUT TO A, B

Step 2. COMPUTE P ← A*B

Step 3. [INITIALISE] R ← 1

Step 4. WHILE R NOT = 0 DO

Step 5. COMPUTE R ← REMAINDER OF (A/B)

Step 6. A ← B

Step 7. B ← R

Step 8. END-WHILE

Step 9. HCF ← A

Step 10. COMPUTE LCM ← P/HCF

(*ii*) COMPUTE S ← S*10 + R

[Increase the previously reversed integer representation S by a factor 10 and add it to the most recently extracted digit to obtain the current value of S]

(*iii*) COMPUTE N ← integer part of (N/10)

[Use the integer division by 10 to remove the right-most digit from the number being reversed]

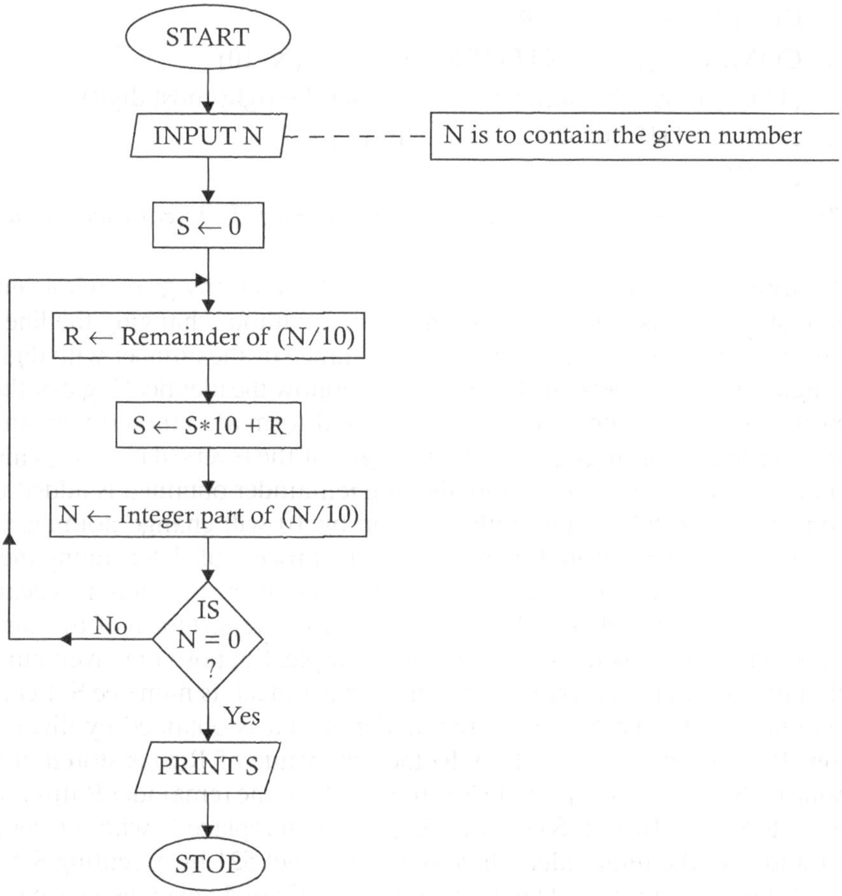

Step 4. PRINT "THE REVERSED VALUE OF", N, "IS", S

Step 5. STOP

Problem 3.21. *Construct a flowchart to show how the divisors of a given number can be obtained.*

Task Analysis. A number is called a divisor of another number if the division of the latter by the former leaves zero as remainder. Usually, the whole numbers starting from 1 are taken as divisors. The divisors are also known as factors of the number. To obtain all the divisors of a number, we need to start testing from 1 until we reach the half of the number after which only the number itself remains as its divisor. The following flowchart shows the procedure.

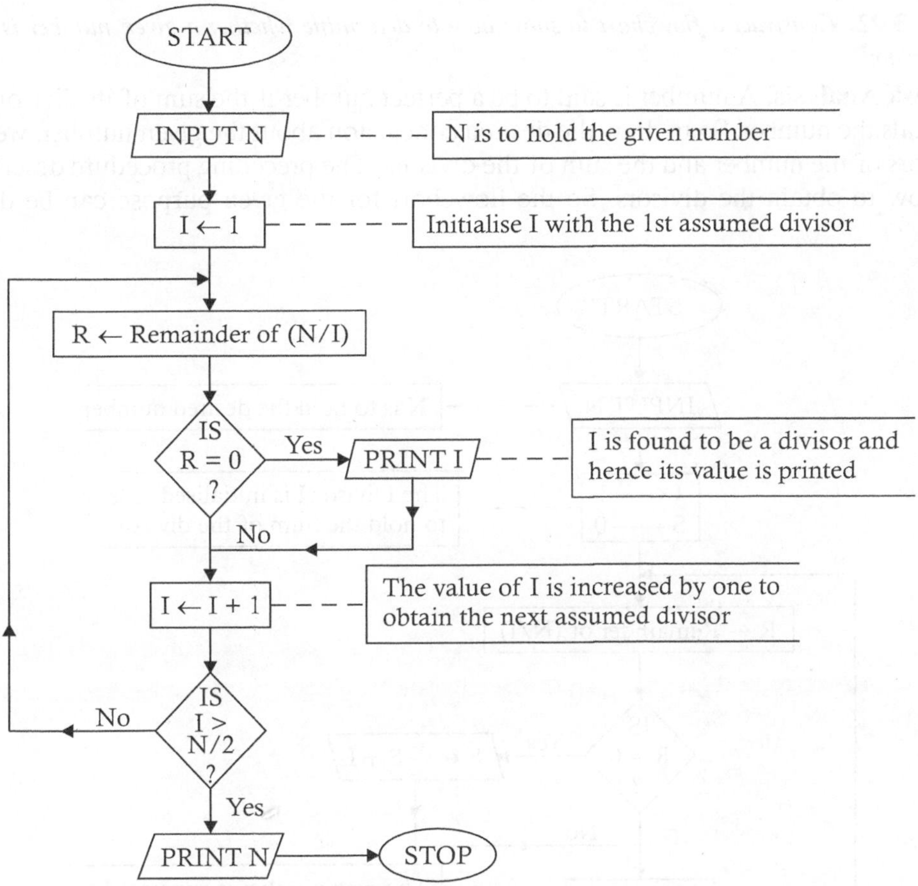

The solution to the above problem has been shown through the following algorithm :

Step 1. INPUT TO N
[ACCEPT the number the divisors of which are to be obtained and store it in N]

Step 2. [Set the initial value of the divisor]
I ← 1

Step 3. While I <= integer part of (N/2) DO
(*i*) COMPUTE R ← REMAINDER OF (N/I)
(*ii*) IF R = 0
THEN PRINT I
END-IF
(*iii*) COMPUTE I ← I + 1
[Increment the value of the divisor]

Step 4. PRINT N
[This is to print the last divisor]

Step 5. STOP

Problem 3.22. *Construct a flowchart to show how to determine whether a given number is a perfect number or not.*

Task Analysis. A number is said to be a perfect number if the sum of its divisors except itself equals the number. So to draw the desired conclusion about the given number, we require the divisors of the number and the sum of the divisors. The preceding procedure describes and shows how to obtain the divisors. So the flowchart for the given purpose can be drawn as under.

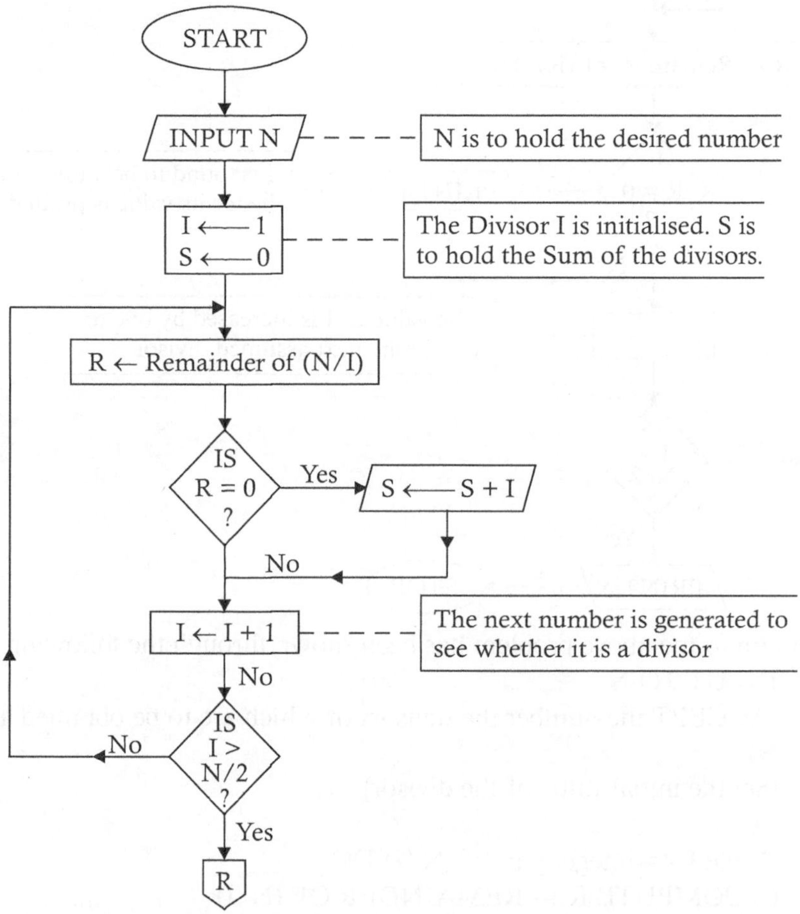

The following algorithm depicts the desired set of steps leading to the solution:

Step 1. INPUT TO N
[ACCEPT THE DESIRED INTEGER AND STORE IT]

Step 2. [INITIALISE THE DIVISOR LOCATION I & THE LOCATION S TO CONTAIN THE SUM OF THE DIVISORS]

Step 3. WHILE I <= Integer part of (N/2) DO
(*i*) COMPUTE R ← REMAINDER OF (N/I)
(*ii*) IF R = 0

THEN COMPUTE S ← S + I
[ACCUMULATE THE DIVISOR OBTAINED]
END-IF
(*iii*) COMPUTE I ← I + 1
[INCREMENT I TO SEE WHETHER IT IS THE NEXT DIVISOR]

Step 4. If S = N
THEN PRINT N, "IS A PERFECT NO."
ELSE
PRINT N, "IS NOT A PERFECT NO."
END-IF

Step 5. STOP

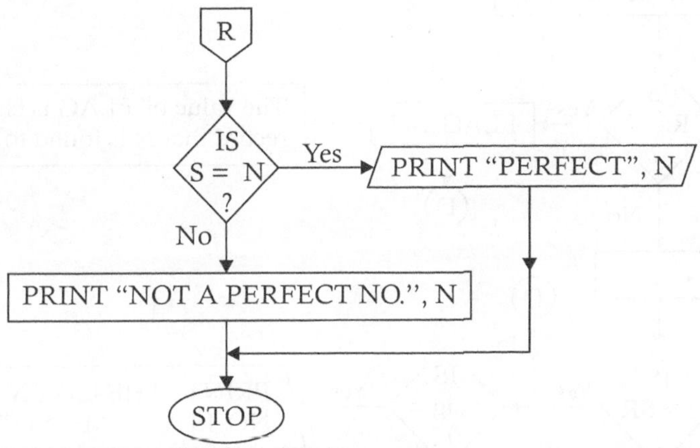

Problem 3.23. *Construct a flowchart to show how you can decide if a given number is prime or not.*

Task Analysis. We know that a number can be called a prime number if and only if it has no divisor or factor except itself and unity *i.e.*, 1. So in order to declare that a number is a prime number, we need to prove that the number is not divisible by any number starting from 2 to the half of the given number because we have already seen that if a number has some divisor at all, it must lie within the half of the number. A better and more efficient strategy is to limit the checking within the integer part of the square root of the number. For example, to check if the number 97 is a prime number or not we need check whether there exists some divisor of 97 within 2 to 48 (both inclusive). This checking can be done from 2 to 9 because 9 is the integer part of the square root of 97. So the number of checking is decreased to a large extent. The divisors can be generated automatically by changing the value of a variable location. Assuming that the procedure for determining the square root of a number is available, the flowchart for the task can be drawn as follows :

The following algorithm shows the steps leading to the desired solution :

Step 1. INPUT TO N
[ACCEPT THE NUMBER WHOSE SQUARE ROOT IS TO BE FOUND OUT]

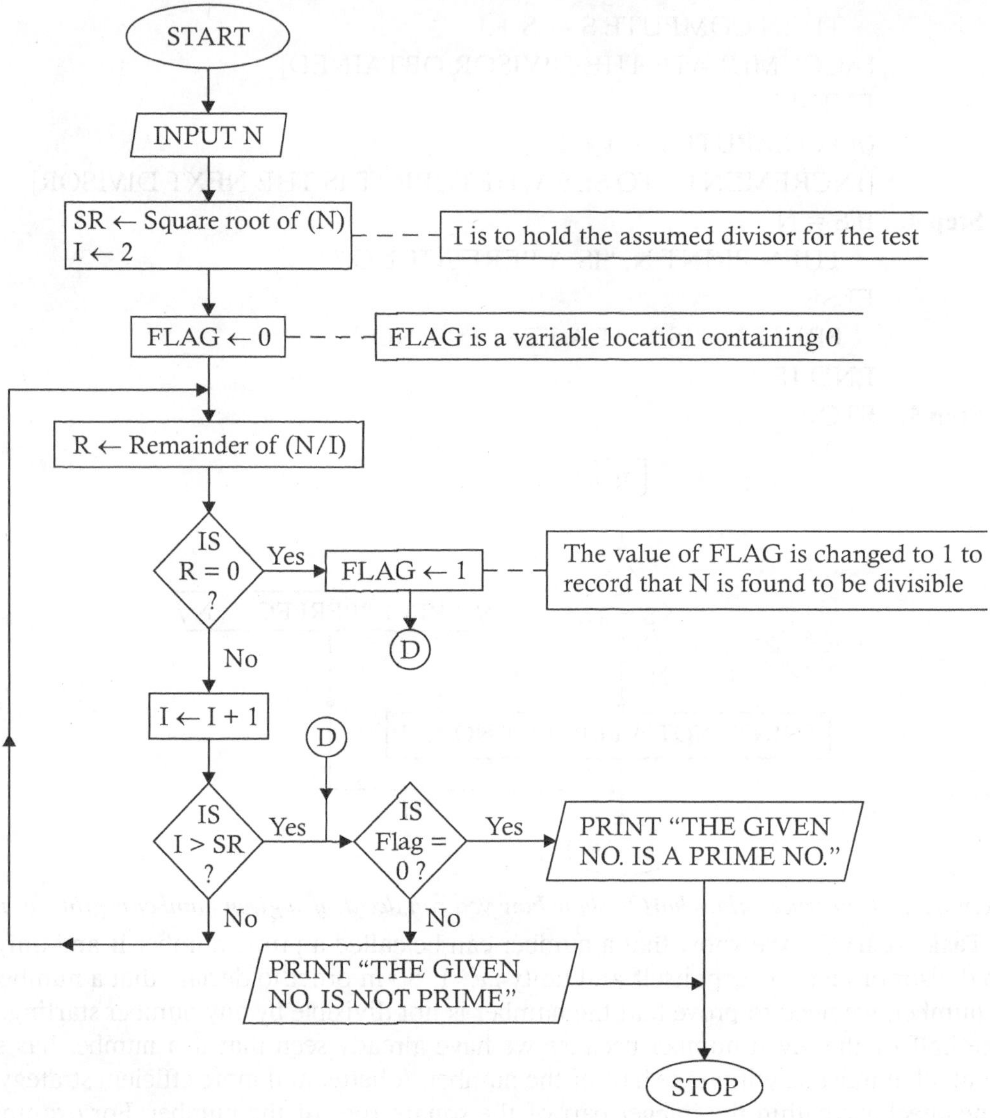

Step 2. COMPUTE SR ← SQUARE ROOT OF (N)

Step 3. [INITIALISE] I ← 2, FLAG ← 0
[FLAG is to contain the divisibility status of the number]

Step 4. WHILE I <= SR DO
(*i*) COMPUTE R ← REMAINDER OF (N/I)
(*ii*) IF R = 0
THEN FLAG ← 1
EXIT
END-IF

(*iii*) COMPUTE I ← I + 1
(Increment I to obtain the next divisor]

Step 5. IF FLAG = 0
THEN PRINT "It is a Prime No."
ELSE
PRINT "It is not a Prime No."
END-IF

Step 6. STOP

Problem 3.24. *Construct a flowchart to show the logic of printing first N Fibonacci numbers. Fibonacci numbers are obtained from the relationship* $t_i = t_{i-1} + t_{i-2}$, *i = 2 to n where* $t_o = 0$, $t_1 = 1$.

Task Analysis. From the given relationship, it is clear that any Fibonacci number can be obtained by taking the sum of the preceding two numbers. For example, third Fibonacci number can be obtained by taking the sum of the first two *i.e.* 0 + 1 = 1 ; the fourth Fibonacci number

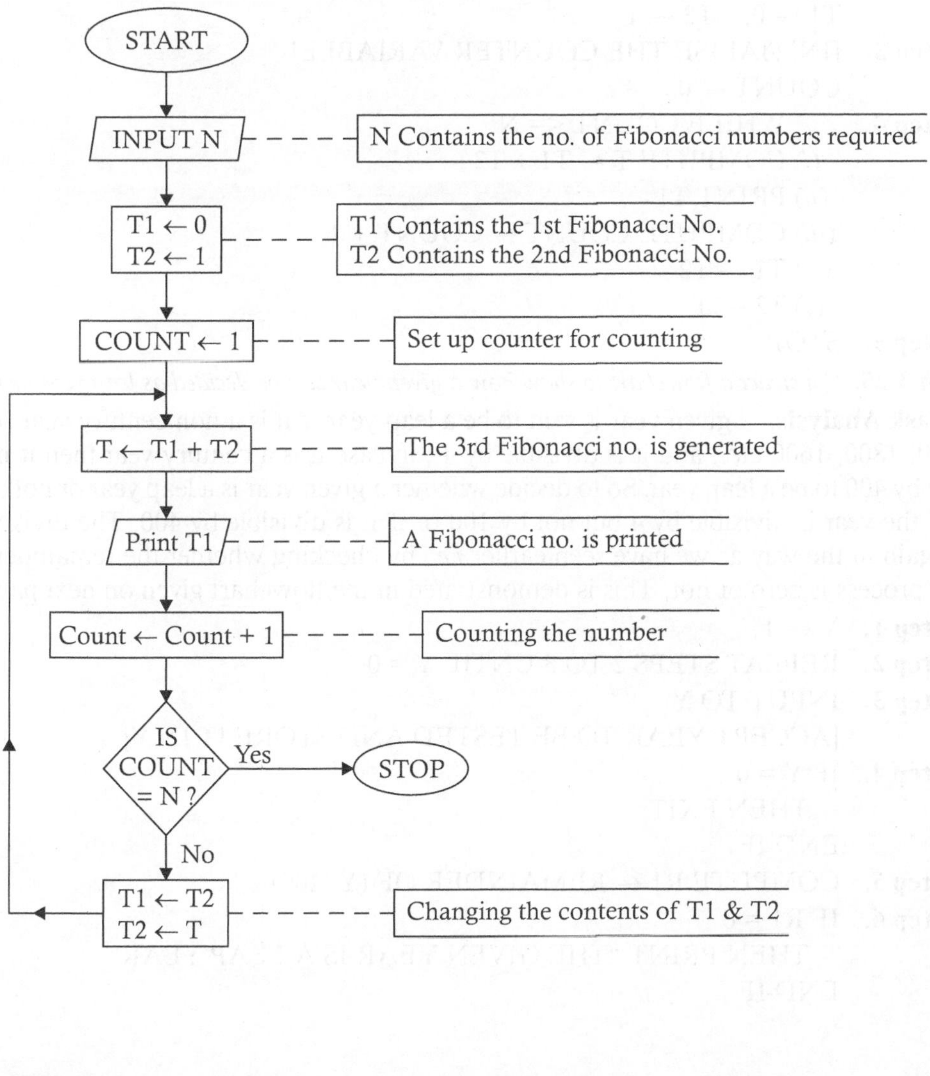

can be obtained by taking the sum of the 2nd and the 3rd number *i.e.*, 1 + 1 = 2 and so on ; hence a simple expression of the form C = A + B can be built and used to generate the Fibonacci numbers, where A and B will initially represent the first two Fibonacci numbers and C the 3rd one. Having obtained the 3rd Fibonacci number, we can assign the value of B to A and that of C to B to get the 2nd and the 3rd Fibonacci numbers in A and B and then using the expression (*i.e.*, C = A + B), we can derive the fourth Fibonacci number. This procedure of assigning the value of B to A and C to B to get the next Fibonacci number, can be repeated any number times until the desired numbers are obtained. A counter may be maintained to count the numbers printed. This is shown in the flowchart above.

The algorithm below shows the solution of the above problem.

Step 1. INPUT TO N
[Establish N, the number of FIBONACCI NUMBERS to be generated]

Step 2. [INITIALISE VARIABLES WITH THE FIRST TWO FIBONACCI NUMBERS]
T1 ← 0, T2 ← 1

Step 3. [INITIALISE THE COUNTER VARIABLE]
COUNT ← 0

Step 4. WHILE COUNT <= N
(*i*) COMPUTE T ← T1 + T2
(*ii*) PRINT T1
(*iii*) COMPUTE COUNT ← COUNT + 1
(*iv*) T1 ← T2
(*v*) T2 ← T

Step 5. STOP

Problem 3.25. *Construct a flowchart to show how a given year can be decided as leap year or not.*

Task Analysis. A given year is said to be a leap year if it is a non-century year (*i.e.*, not like 1900, 1800, 1600 etc.) and it is divisible by 4 ; in case it is a century year then it must be divisible by 400 to be a leap year. So to decide whether a given year is a leap year or not ; we are to see if the year is divisible by 4 but not by 100 or if it is divisible by 400. The divisibility is tested again in the way as we have seen earlier *i.e.*, by checking whether the remainder in the division process is zero or not. This is demonstrated in the flowchart given on next page.

Step 1. Y ← 1

Step 2. REPEAT STEPS 2 TO 8 UNTIL Y = 0

Step 3. INPUT TO Y
[ACCEPT YEAR TO BE TESTED AND STORE IT IN Y]

Step 4. IF Y = 0
THEN EXIT
END-IF

Step 5. COMPUTE R1 ← REMAINDER OF (Y/400)

Step 6. IF R1 = 0
THEN PRINT "THE GIVEN YEAR IS A LEAP YEAR"
END-IF

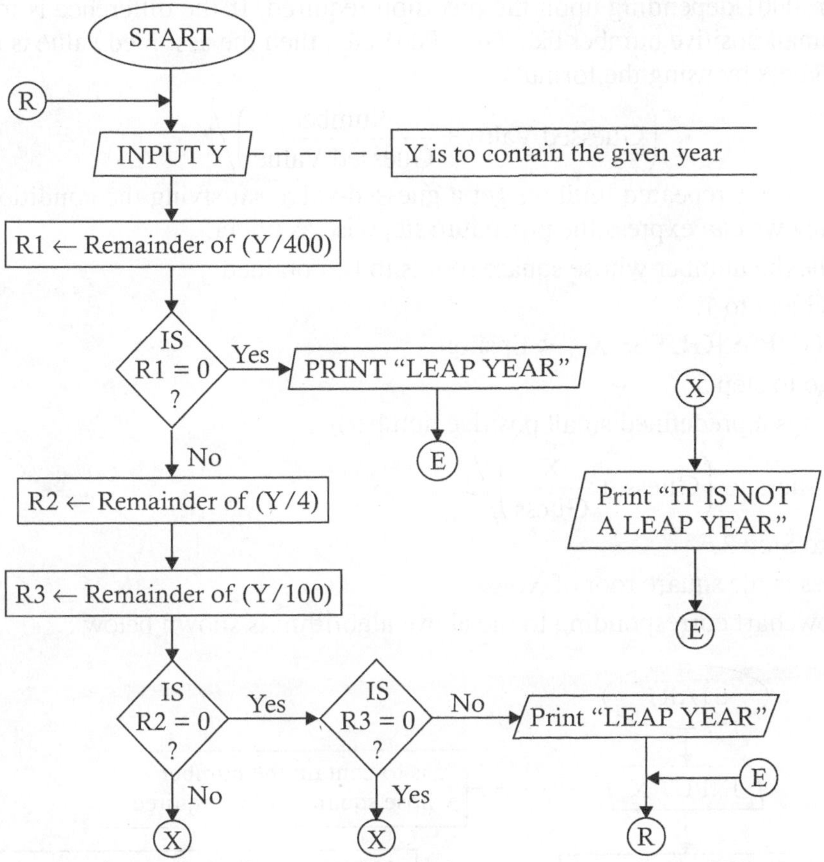

Step 6. COMPUTE R2 ← REMAINDER OF (Y/4)
Step 7. COMPUTE R3 ← REMAINDER OF (Y/100)
Step 8. IF R2 = 0 AND R3 NOT = 0

THEN PRINT "THE GIVEN YEAR IS A LEAP YEAR"

ELSE

PRINT "THE GIVEN YEAR IS NOT A LEAP YEAR"

END-IF

Step 9. STOP

Problem 3.26. *Construct a flowchart to show how the square root of a positive number is determined.*

Task Analysis. The square root of a number can be obtained by using a method known as Newton Raphson Method. In this method, the square root of any positive number is initially set to 1. Then the absolute value of the difference between the square of the assumed square root and the given number is obtained. This value is then compared with some predefined small positive number. This small positive number is set in such a way that an error of magnitude less than that is made acceptable. So if the difference becomes less than the small positive number, the assumed square root is taken as the desired square root. For perfect squares, this difference becomes zero, for others this difference is usually found to be of magnitude less than

.01 or .001 or .0001 depending upon the precision required. If the difference is more than or equal to the small positive number like .001, .0001 etc., then the assumed value is increased to have a better guess by using the formula :

$$\left(\text{Guessed Value} + \frac{\text{Number}}{\text{Guessed Value}}\right)\Big/2$$

and the procedure is repeated until we get a guessed value satisfying the condition specified. Algorithmically we can express the procedure stepwise as under.

Let X be the number whose square root is to be obtained.

1. Set Guess to 1.
2. If | GUESS*GUESS-X | < Epsilon
   Then go to step 5
   (Epsilon is a predefined small positive number)
3. Set Guess to $\left(\text{Guess} + \frac{X}{\text{Guess}}\right)\Big/2$
4. Go to Step 2
5. Guess is the square root of X.

The flowchart corresponding to the above algorithm is shown below :

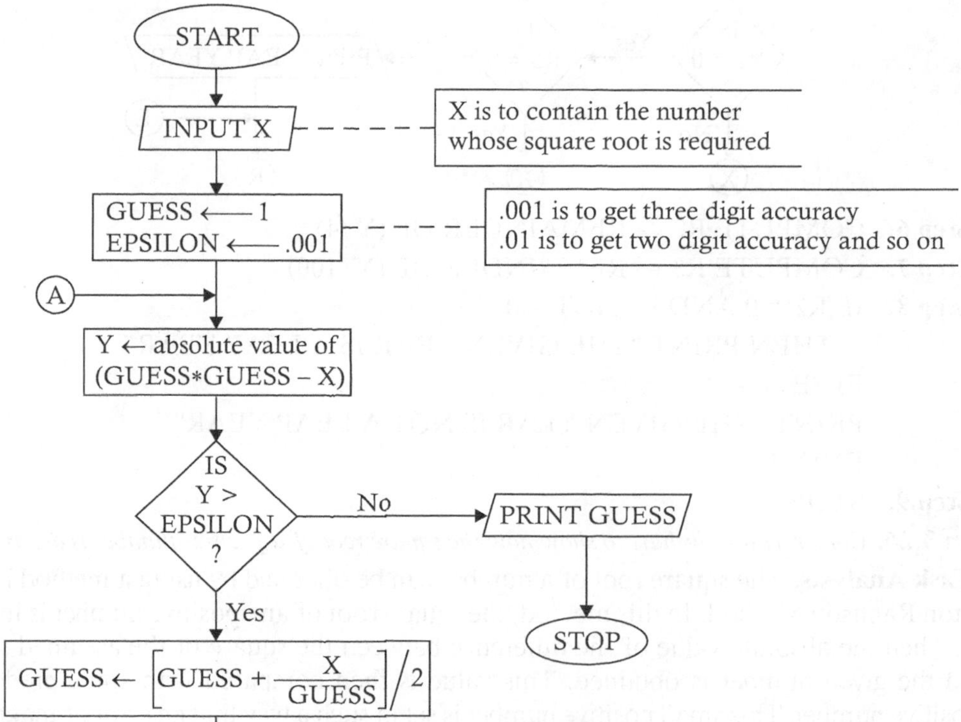

The algorithm for the solution of the above problem is given below :

Step 1. INPUT TO X

Step 2. [INITIALISE] GUESS ← 1, EPSILON ← .001

Step 3. WHILE absolute value of (GUESS*GUESS – X) <= EPSILON DO

$$\text{COMPUTE GUESS} \leftarrow \left(\text{GUESS} + \frac{\text{X}}{\text{GUESS}}\right)\Big/2$$

Step 4. PRINT "THE SQUARE ROOT IS", GUESS

Step 5. STOP

Problem 3.27. *The registration charge of a parcel is determined according to the following rules:*

For the 1st 10 gms, the charge is Rs. 12.75 ;

For the next every 8 gm or part thereof the charge is Rs. 11.25.

Draw a flowchart to show how the registration charge is determined.

Task Analysis. Note that the input required here is the weight of the parcel to be registered. The calculation of the charge requires determining whether the weight lies within 10 gms. or not ; if not then the excess weight beyond 10 gms is to be computed and the number of 8 gms intervals for the excess weight is to be obtained for which the charge is calculated at Rs. 11.25 per interval. The number of 8 gms intervals can be computed by dividing the excess weight by 8 ; if the division leaves zero remainder then the quotient will be the number of intervals. If the division leaves some other remainder then the number of intervals will be the quotient plus 1. The calculation of the number of intervals can, however, be done by using the following formula also : Number of intervals = integer part of (Excess Weight – 1)/8 + 1. The logic is depicted in the flowchart given on next page :

```
Step 1.  REPEAT STEPS 2 THROUGH 6
Step 2.  INPUT TO W
Step 3.  IF W = 0
            THEN EXIT
         END-IF
Step 4.  IF W <= 10
            THEN CHARGE ← 12.75
         ELSE
            COMPUTE EW ← W – 10
            COMPUTE R ← REMAINDER OF (EW/8)
            IF R = 0
               THEN COMPUTE INV ← Integer part of (EW/8)
            ELSE
            COMPUTE INV ← Integer part of (EW/8) + 1
               END-IF
         END-IF
```

```
Step 3.  IF W <= 0
            THEN EXIT
         END-IF
Step 4.  IF W <= 40
            THEN CHG ← 5.75
         ELSE IF W <= 500
               THEN COMPUTE EW ← W – 40
               COMPUTE INV ← Integer part of ((EW – 1)/18) + 1
               COMPUTE CHG ← 5.75 + INV*3.88
            ELSE
            COMPUTE CHG ← 5.75 + 26*3.88 + (W – 500)*0.67
            END-IF
         END-IF
Step 5.  PRINT "THE CHARGE IS RS.", CHG
Step 6.  STOP
```

Problem 3.29. *Construct a flowchart for obtaining the sum of a given number of terms (N) for a given value of x in the following mathematical series :*

$$X + X^2/2 + X^3/3 + \ldots\ldots \text{ upto } N \text{ terms.}$$

Task Analysis. Here we observe that we need to know the values of two unknown quantities as input, namely, the value of X and that of N, the number of terms. Next we are to find out a general expression from which we can find out different terms. The expression X/I will yield different terms for different values of I from 1 to N. So, we can evaluate the expression for some given value of X and the obtained value can be stored in some location, say S, that initially contains 0. Successive addition of the evaluated values for all the terms to the content of S will give us the desired sum. This is shown in the flowchart given on next page.

The algorithm leading to the solution of the above problem has been shown below :

```
Step 1.  REPEAT STEPS 2 THROUGH 10 WHILE USER LIKES
Step 2.  INPUT TO X
         [ACCEPT THE VALUE OF THE UNKNOWN X FROM THE TERMINAL
         AND STORE IT IN X]
Step 3.  IF X <= 0
            THEN STOP
         END-IF
Step 4.  INPUT TO N
         [ACCEPT THE NUMBER OF TERMS TO BE ADDED AND STORE IT
         IN N]
```

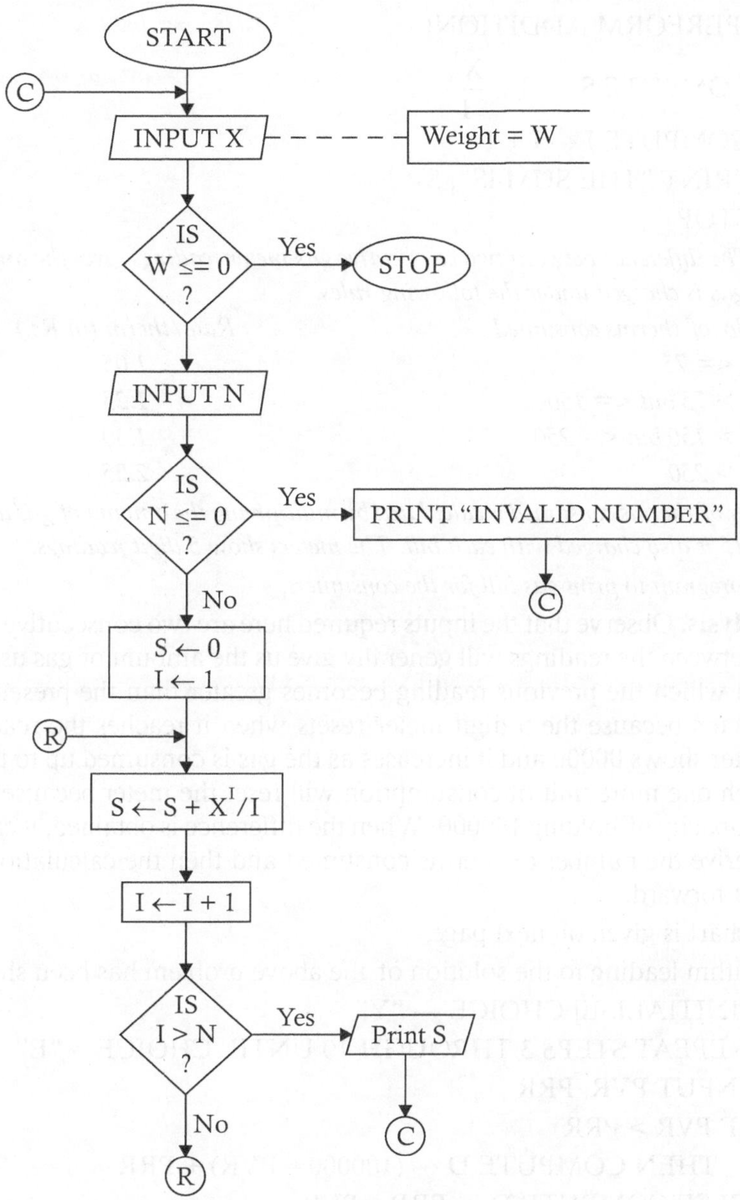

Step 5. IF N <= 0
THEN PRINT "INVALID NUMBER"
CONTINUE FROM STEP 2
END-IF

Step 6. [INITIALISE REQUIRED LOCATIONS]
$S \leftarrow 0, I \leftarrow 1$

Step 7. WHILE I <= N REPEAT STEPS 8 AND 9

Step 8. [PERFORM ADDITION]

COMPUTE $S \leftarrow S + \dfrac{X^I}{I}$

Step 9. COMPUTE I ← I + 1

Step 10. PRINT "THE SUM IS", S

Step 11. STOP

Problem 3.30. *The difference between two consecutive gas meter readings gives the amount of gas used in cubic feet. The gas is charged under the following rules.*

No. of therms consumed	*Rate/therm (in Rs.)*
<= 75	*1.05*
> 75 but <= 150	*1.25*
> 150 but <= 250	*1.50*
> 250	*2.25*

The number of therms consumed is calculated by multiplying the amount of gas used by 1.06748. A meter rent of Rs. 15 is also charged with each bill. The meters show 5 digit readings.

Develop a program to print gas bill for the consumers.

Task Analysis. Observe that the inputs required here are two consecutive meter readings. The difference between the readings will generally give us the amount of gas used except in the extreme cases in which the previous reading becomes greater than the present reading. This extreme case occurs because the 5 digit meter resets when it reaches the reading of 100000 (initially, the meter shows 00000 and it increases as the gas is consumed up to the largest value 99999 after which one more unit of consumption will reset the meter because the meter does not possess the capacity of holding 100000. When the difference is obtained, it can be multiplied by 1.06748 to derive the number of therms consumed and then the calculation of the charge becomes straight forward.

The flowchart is given on next page.

The algorithm leading to the solution of the above problem has been shown below :

Step 1. [INITIALISE] CHOICE ← "Y"

Step 2. REPEAT STEPS 3 THROUGH 10 UNTIL CHOICE = "E"

Step 3. INPUT PVR, PRR

Step 4. IF PVR > PRR

THEN COMPUTE D ← (100000 – PVR) + PRR

ELSE COMPUTE D ← PRR – PVR

END-IF

Step 5. COMPUTE TH ← D∗1.06748

Step 6. IF TH <= 75

THEN COMPUTE CHARGE ← TH∗1.05 + 15

ELSE IF TH <= 150

THEN COMPUTE CHARGE ← TH∗1.25 + 15

ELSE IF TH <= 250

THEN COMPUTE CHARGE ← TH∗1.50 + 15

ELSE COMPUTE CHARGE ← TH*2.25 + 15
END-IF
END-IF
END-IF

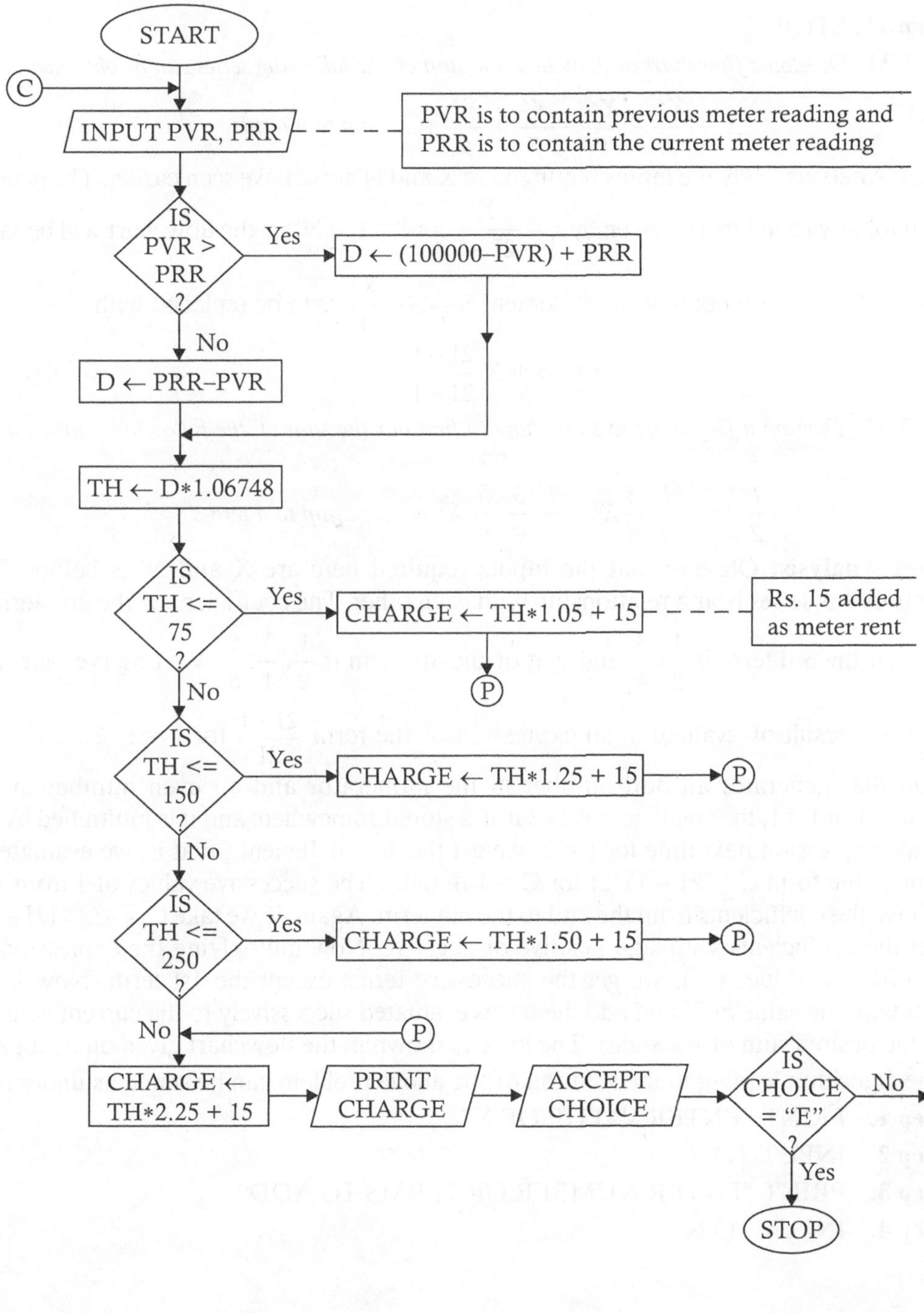

Step 7. PRINT "THE CHARGE IS", CHARGE

Step 8. PRINT "TO TERMINATE ENTER 'E' ELSE PRESS ANY OTHER KEY"

Step 9. ACCEPT CHOICE

Step 10. IF CHOICE = "E" THEN EXIT
END-IF

Step 11. STOP

Problem 3.31. *Develop a flowchart to show how the sum of the following series can be obtained* :

$$X - \frac{X^3}{3} + \frac{X^5}{5} - \frac{X^7}{7} + \frac{X^9}{9} \mp ...... \text{ up to } n \text{ terms}$$

Task Analysis. Here the inputs required are X and N as we have seen earlier. The general expression for any term I can be given by $t_I = \frac{X}{2I-1}$ for I = 1 to N. So the flowchart will be same as that for problem 40 except that the statement $S \leftarrow S + \frac{X^I}{I}$ is to be replaced with

$$S \leftarrow S + X\frac{2I-1}{2I-1}$$

Problem 3.32. *Develop a flowchart to show how to find out the sum of the following mathematical series :*

$$X - \frac{1}{2}X^3 + \frac{1}{2}.\frac{3}{4}X^5 - \frac{1}{2}.\frac{3}{4}.\frac{5}{6}X^7 + ... \text{ up to } n \text{ terms}$$

Task Analysis. Observe that the inputs required here are X and N as before. The coefficients in this series bear a relationship with each other. The coefficient of the 2nd term is $\frac{1}{2}$ and that of the 3rd term is $\frac{1}{2}.\frac{3}{4}$ and that of the 4th term is $\frac{1}{2}.\frac{3}{4}.\frac{5}{6}$. We observe that each coefficient is a result of evaluating an expression of the form $\frac{2I-1}{2I}$ for I = 1, 2 ...., an expression that generates an odd number in the numerator and an even number in the denominator. For I = 1, the coefficient is 1/2 if it is stored somewhere and it is multiplied by the value of the expression next time for I = 2, we get the 3rd coefficient ; that is, we evaluate an expression of the form C * (21 – 1)/2I for C = 1 initially. The successive values of I from 1 to $n-1$ will give the coefficients from the 2nd to the nth term. Again, if we take C = – C * (2I – 1)/ 2I, we get the coefficients with sign positive or negative. Now multiplying the expression by X^{2I+1} for different values of I, we get the successive terms except the 1st term. Now if we initialise S with the value of X and add the terms evaluated successively to the current value of S, we get the desired sum of the series. The logic is shown in the flowchart given on next page.

The algorithm leading to the solution of the above problem can be stated as under :

Step 1. PRINT "ENTER VALUE OF X"

Step 2. INPUT TO X

Step 3. PRINT "ENTER NUMBER OF TERMS TO ADD"

Step 4. INPUT TO N

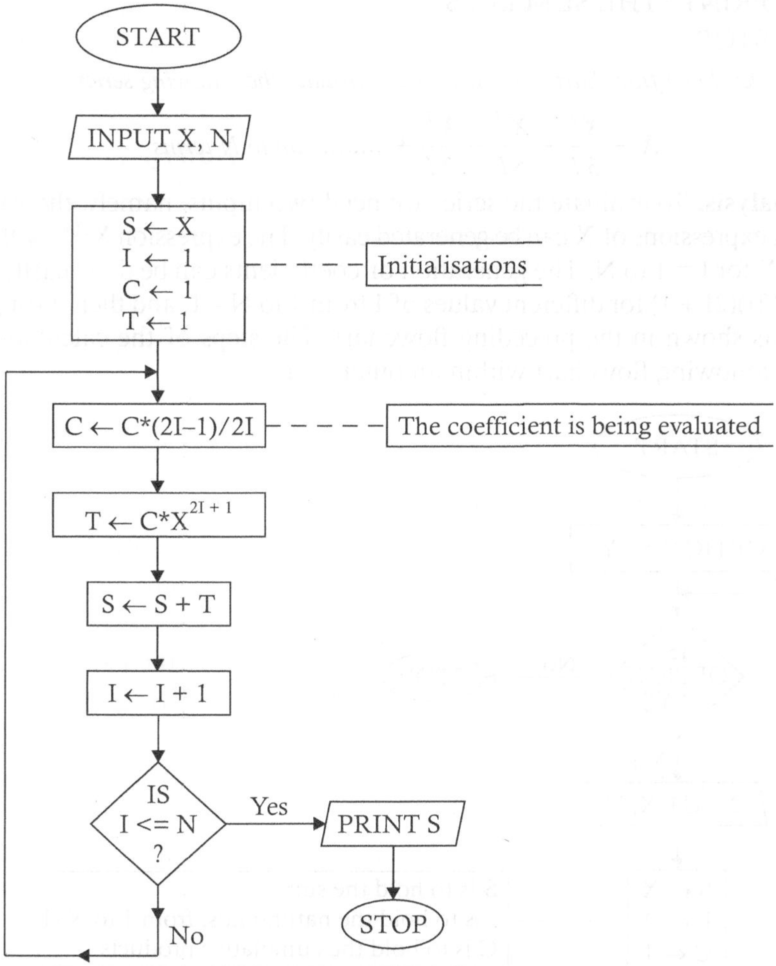

Step 5. [INITIALISE SUM ACCUMULATOR, LOOP VARIABLE, COEFFICIENT & TERM VARIABLE RESPECTIVELY]
$S \leftarrow X, I \leftarrow 1, C \leftarrow 1, T \leftarrow 1$

Step 6. REPEAT WHILE I <= N

(*a*) COMPUTE $C \leftarrow -C*(2*I - 1)/(2*I)$
[Obtain the Ith COEFFICIENT]

(*b*) COMPUTE $T \leftarrow C*X^{2*I+1}$
[Obtain the Ith term]

(*c*) COMPUTE $S \leftarrow S + T$
[Obtain the sum of the Ith term]

(*d*) COMPUTE $I \leftarrow I + 1$
[Increment the loop counter]

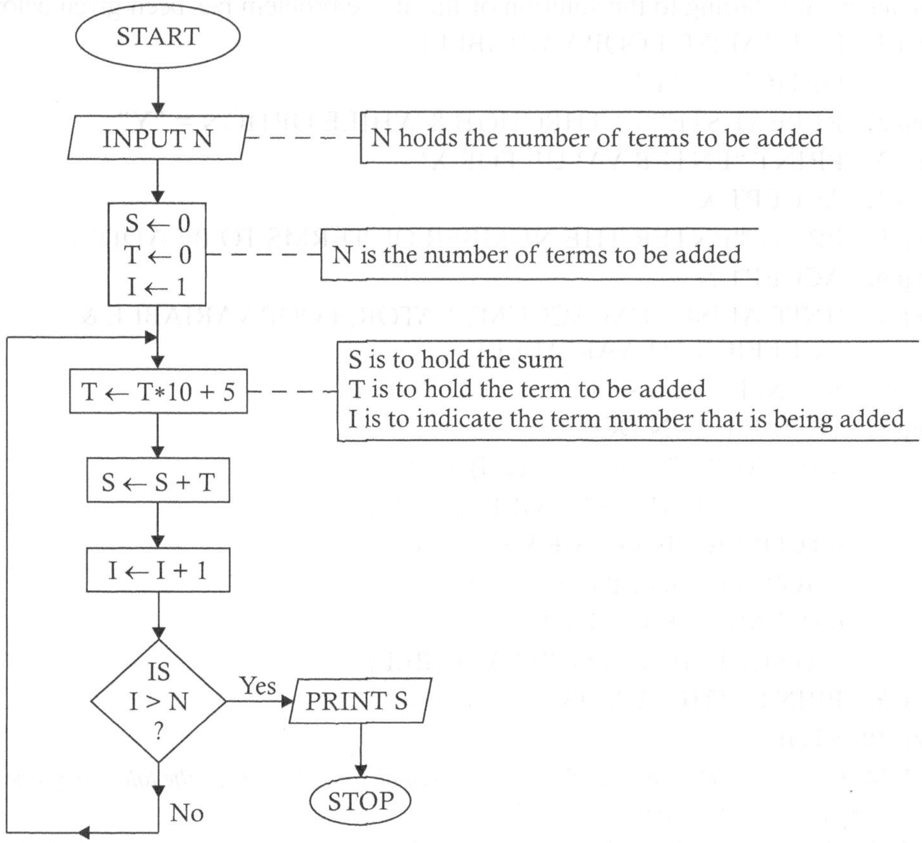

Step 5. PRINT "THE SUM IS", S

Step 6. STOP

Problem 3.35. *Develop a flowchart to show how to find out all perfect numbers within 10 thousand.*

Task Analysis. We have seen earlier how to determine perfect numbers. Here we need to test all the natural numbers within 10000 and to print a number in the range whenever it is found to be perfect. As we know that the first perfect number is 6, so we can start testing numbers from 6. The solution of this problem will require a nested loop. The outer loop is to generate the numbers one by one and the inner loop is to find out the sum of the divisors of each of the generated numbers. Having obtained the sum of the divisors, the number under consideration is to be compared with the resulting sum to decide whether the taken number is perfect or not. If it is found to be a perfect number, the task is to print it and then to transfer the control back to the process of number generation to test the next one unless the highest limit is reached.

The steps of the solution have been depicted in the following flowchart :

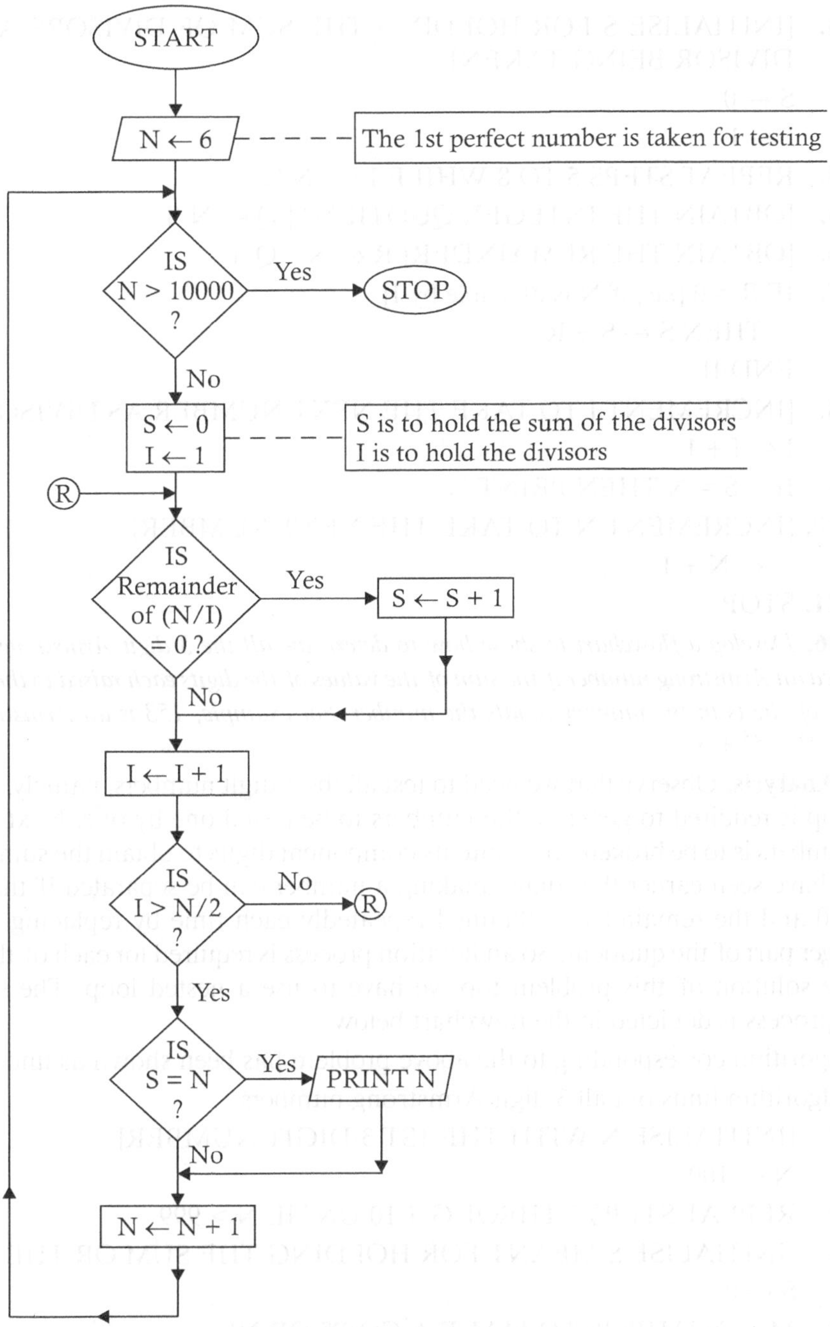

The algorithm corresponding to the above problem has been shown below :

Step 1. [INITIALISE N] N ← 6

Step 2. REPEAT STEPS 3 TO 10 FOR N = 6 TO 10000

Task Analysis. In this problem too we do not require any input from the terminal because we need to test all the three digit numbers as in the preceding problem which can be generated serially. This solution too requires a nested loop. The determination of factorial has been shown earlier. Here the process is to be repeated for each of the digits. The following flowchart shows the steps of the solution :

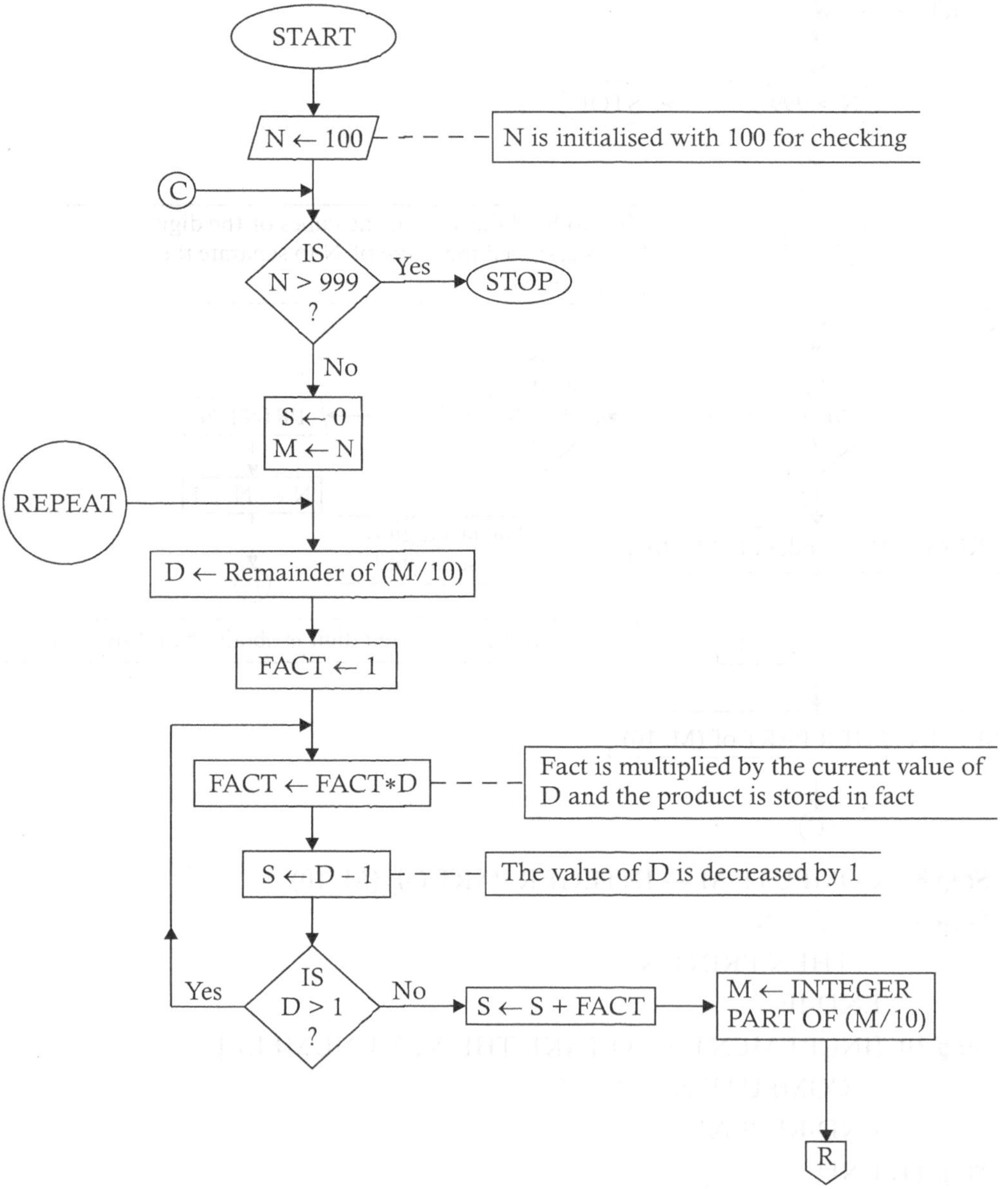

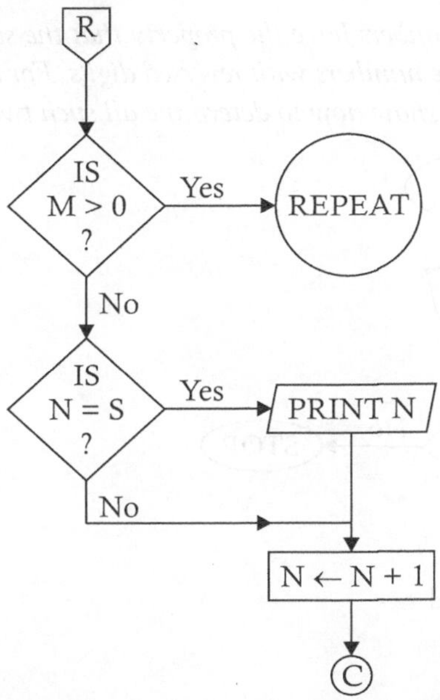

The algorithm corresponding to the above problem is given below :

This algorithm is to find out all the 3-digit numbers for which the sum of the factorials of the digits equals the number.

Step 1. [INITIALISE N WITH THE 1ST 3-DIGIT NUMBER]
$N \leftarrow 100$

Step 2. REPEAT STEPS 3 THROUGH STEP 15 UNTIL $N > 999$

Step 3. [INITIALISE S MEANT FOR HOLDING THE SUM OR THE CUBES]
$S \leftarrow 0$

Step 4. [MAKE A COPY OF N] $M \leftarrow N$

Step 5. REPEAT STEP 6 THROUGH STEP 13 WHILE $M > 0$

Step 6. COMPUTE $D \leftarrow$ REMAINDER OF (M/10)

Step 7. [INITIALISE] FACT ← 1

Step 8. REPEAT WHILE $D > 1$

Step 9. COMPUTE FACT ← FACT∗D

Step 10. COMPUTE $D \leftarrow D - 1$ [DECREMENT D]

Step 11. END-WHILE

Step 12. COMPUTE S ← S + FACT

Step 13. COMPUTE M ← INTEGER PART OF (M/10)

Step 14. IF $N = S$
THEN PRINT N
END-IF

Step 15. [INCREMENT N TO TAKE THE NEXT 3-DIGIT NO.]
COMPUTE $N \leftarrow N + 1$

Step 16. END

Problem 3.38. *Some two digit numbers have the property that the sum of the squares of the numbers equals the sum of the squares of the numbers with reversed digits. For example,* $48^2 + 52^2 + 63^2 = 84^2 + 25^2 + 36^2$*, construct a flowchart to show how to determine all such two digit numbers.*

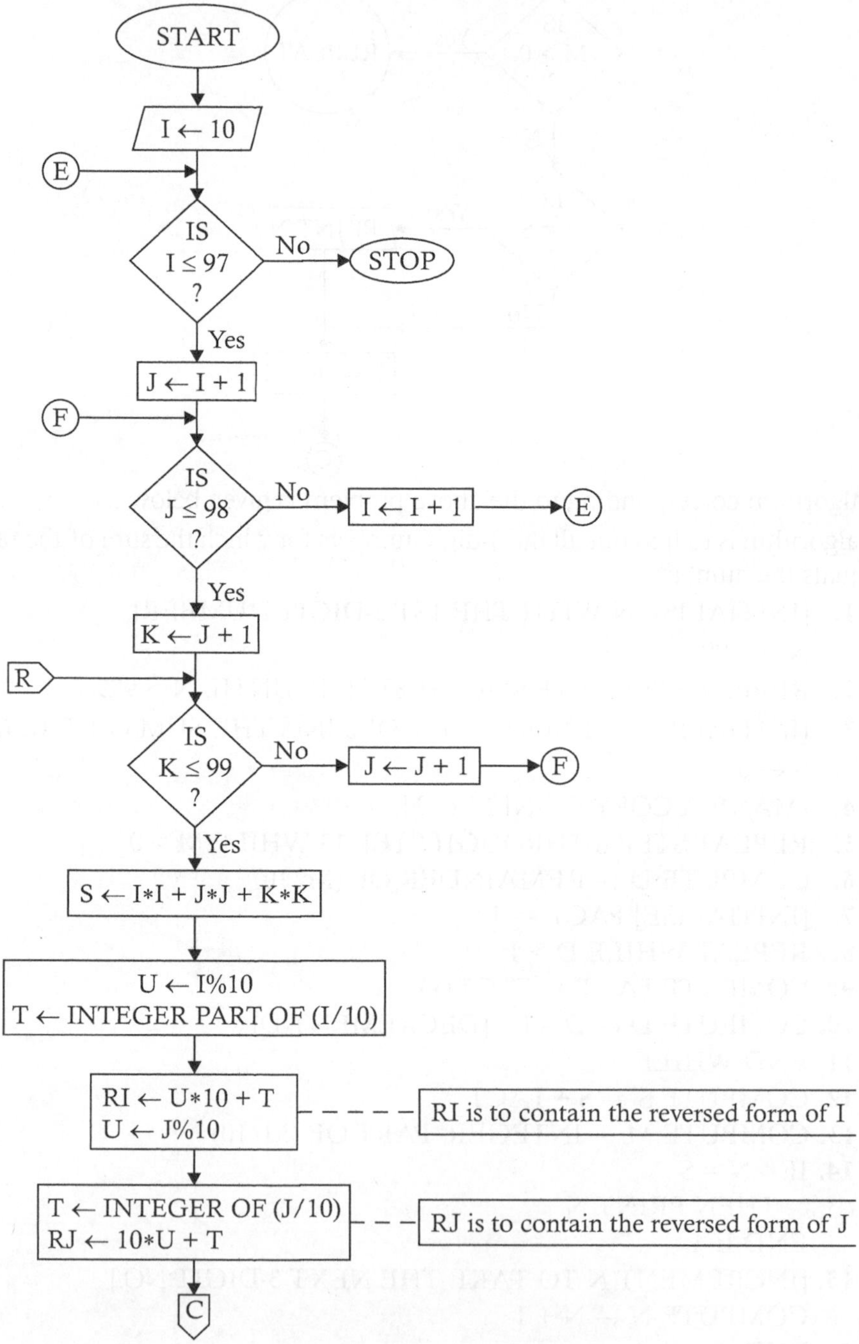

Task Analysis. Observe that the solution of this problem requires the checking of all two digit triplets. Such that the triplet satisfies the specified property with no number repeated. The repetition of a number can be prevented by establishing three nested loops. The 1st loop is to generate numbers from 10 to 97. The next inner loop is to generate numbers from 11 to 98 and the next inner loop is to generate numbers from 12 to 99 such that the 1st triplet to be tested is 10, 11, 12 the next tripped is 10.11, 13 and so on. The next task is to obtain the sum of the squares of the numbers with digits reversed. To obtain a number with digits reversed, we separate the digits of the unit's place and that of the ten's place then we use the formula : digit of the unit's place * 10 + Digit of the ten's place. The steps of the computation have been shown above.

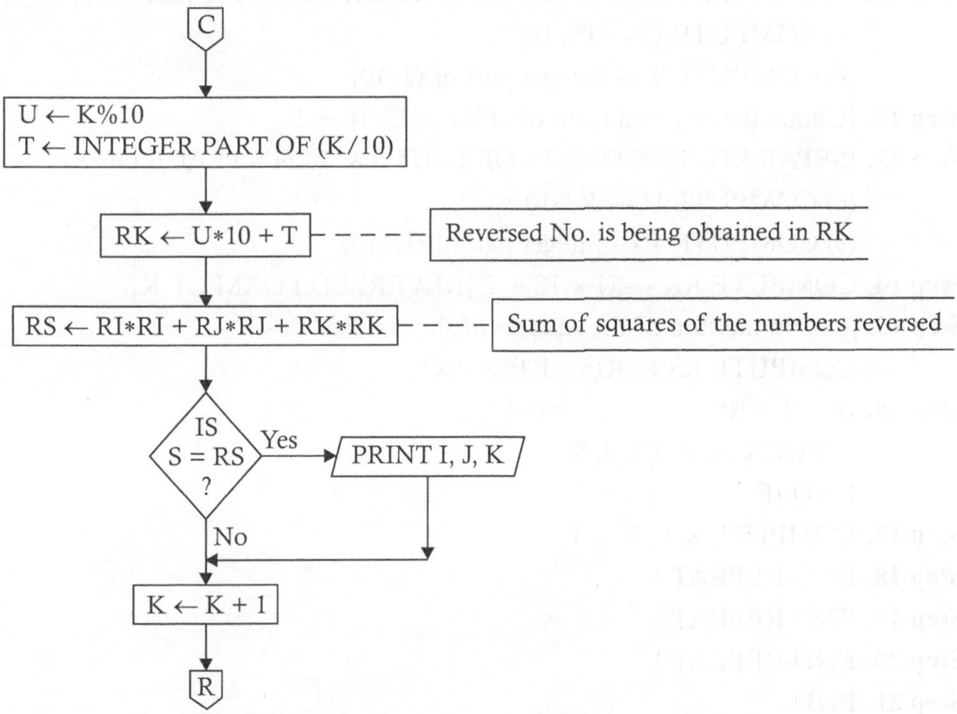

The algorithm corresponding to the above solution strategy will be as under :

Step 1. [Initialise the Ist loop variable]

I ← 10

Step 2. REPEAT STEPS 3 TO 19 WHILE I <= 97

Step 3. [Initialise the 2nd loop variable]

J ← I + 1

Step 4. REPEAT STEPS 5 TO 18 WHILE J <= 98

Step 5. [Initialise the 3rd loop variable]

K ← J + 1

Step 6. REPEAT STEPS 7 TO 17 WHILE K <= 99

Step 7. [CALCULATE SUM OF THE SQUARES OF THE 1ST 3 NOS. REPRESENTED BY THE LOOP VARIABLES]

Step 8. COMPUTE S ← $I^2 + J^2 + K^2$

Step 9. [SEPARATE THE DIGITS OF UNIT'S & TEN'S PLACE OF I]

(*a*) COMPUTE U ← I% 10 [DIVIDE I BY 10 & COLLECT THE REMAINDER]

(*b*) COMPUTE T ← Integer part of (I/10)

Step 10. [Obtain the reversed form of I] COMPUTE RI ← U*10 + T

Step 11. [SEPARATE THE DIGITS OF UNIT'S & TEN'S PLACE OF J]

(*a*) COMPUTE U ← J% 10

(*b*) COMPUTE T ← Integer part of (J/10)

Step 12. [Obtain the reversed form of J] RJ ← U*10 + T

Step 13. [SEPARATE THE DIGITS OF UNIT'S & TEN'S PLACE OF K]

(*a*) COMPUTE U ← K%10

(*b*) COMPUTE T ← Integer part of (K/10)

Step 14. COMPUTE RK ← U × 10 + T [REVERSED FORM OF K]

Step 15. [Obtain the sum of the squares of the reversed nos.]

COMPUTE RS ← $RI^2 + RJ^2 + RK^2$

Step 16. IF R = RS

THEN PRINT I, J, K

END-IF

Step 17. COMPUTE K ← K + 1

Step 18. END-REPEAT K

Step 19. END-REPEAT J

Step 20. END-REPEAT I

Step 21. END

Problem 3.39. *It is required to determine the difference between two given dates. Construct a flowchart to show how to do it.*

Task Analysis. The inputs required here are day, month and year number of two dates. The difference between the dates can then be computed by comparing the day-numbers first and then by taking the difference ; the month numbers are then compared and the number of months in between is then obtained. Now, when two day numbers are compared, the day number of the smaller date may be larger than that of the greater date ; then to obtain the number of days in the difference, we add 30 to the smaller day number and subtract 1 from the corresponding month number ; otherwise the number of days in the difference can be obtained through outright subtraction. To obtain the number of months in the difference, we compare the month number in the larger date with that in the smaller date. If the month number in the larger date is smaller than that of the smaller date then 12 is added to the corresponding month number and then the number of months in the difference can be obtained through subtraction and 1 is subtracted from the year number of the larger date ; otherwise the number of months can be obtained through straightforward subtraction.

There will be no such problem in obtaining the number of years because the year in the larger date will always be larger than the year in the smaller date. The procedure is depicted below through flowchart.

The algorithm corresponding to the above problem is stated below :

Step 1. Set WISH to TRUE

Step 2. Repeat steps 3 to 12 WHILE WISH

Step 3. Accept day (DD), month (MM) and year (YY) component of the larger date

Step 4. Accept day (DD1), month (MM1) and year (YY1) component of the smaller date

Step 5. IF DD < DD1

THEN COMPUTE DD ← DD + 30

COMPUTE MM ← MM – 1

END-IF

Step 6. COMPUTE D ← DD – DD1

Step 7. IF MM < MM1

THEN COMPUTE MM ← MM + 12

COMPUTE YY ← YY – 1

END-IF

Step 8. COMPUTE M ← MM – MM1

Step 9. PRINT Y, "YEARS", M, "MONTHS", D, "DAYS"

Step 10. PRINT "CONTINUE? (Y/N)"

Step 11. INPUT TO CHOICE

Step 12. IF CHOICE ! = "Y"

THEN Set WISH to FALSE

END-IF

Step 13. END-WHILE

Step 6. [INCREMENT EACH OF THE VARIABLES REPRESENTING THE NUMBERS]

COMPUTE $I \leftarrow I + 1$

COMPUTE $J \leftarrow J + 1$

COMPUTE $K \leftarrow K + 1$

Step 7. END-REPEAT

Step 8. END

Problem 3.41. *Construct a flowchart to show how number of elapsed days between two dates.*

Task Analysis. The problem is to determine the difference between two dates in number of days. For example, the number of days between July 12, 1985, and July 26, 1985, is obviously 14. But in the determination of number of days between two dates that differ widely, say, February 10, 1969 and July 21, 1988, the calculation is a bit more complex. Luckily, there is a formula that can be used to calculate the number of days between two dates. This is effected by computing the value of N for each of the two dates and then by taking the difference, where N is calculated as follows :

$$N = 1461 \times f(\text{year, month})/4 + 153 \times g\,(\text{month})/5 + \text{days}$$

where :

$$f(\text{year, month}) = \text{year} - 1, \text{ if month} \leq 2$$
$$= \text{year, otherwise}$$
$$g(\text{month}) = \text{month} + 13, \text{ if month} \leq 2$$
$$= \text{month} + 1, \text{ otherwise}$$

and all calculations are performed using integer arithmetic.

As an example of applying the formula, to calculate the number of days between February 10, 1969 and July 21, 1988, we can calculate the values of N_1 and N_2 by substituting the appropriate values into the above formula as shown below.

$$N_1 = 1461 \times f(1969,2)/4 + 153 \times g\,(2)/5 + 10$$
$$= (1461 \times 1968)/4 + 153 \times (2 + 13)/5 + 10$$
$$= 2875248/4 + 2295/5 + 10$$
$$= 718812 + 459 + 10$$
$$= 719281$$
$$N_2 = 1461 \times f(1988,7)/4 + 153 \times g\,(7)/5 + 21$$
$$= (1461 \times 1988)/4 + (153 \times 8)/5 + 21$$
$$= 2904468/4 + 1224/5 + 21$$
$$= 726117 + 244 + 21$$
$$= 726382$$

So the number of elapsed days $= N_2 - N_1 = 719281 - 726382 = 7101$.

So the number of days between the two dates is shown to be 7101. The above formula is applicable for any date after March 1, 1900, (1 must be added to N for dates from March 1,1800 to February 28, 1900, and 2 must be added for dates between March 1, 1700, and

February 28, 1800 and so on). The steps of the solution have been shown in the flowchart below.

The algorithm corresponding to the solution of the above problem has been described below :

Step 1. WISH = "Y"
Step 2. REPEAT Step 3 to Step 12 WHILE WISH = "Y"
Step 3. ACCEPT DATE 1, DATE 2
Step 4. [SEPARATE DAY, MONTH AND YEAR]
DD1 ← Day No. of DATE 1
MM1 ← Month No. of DATE 1
YY1 ← Year No. of DATE 1
DD2 ← Day No. of DATE 2
MM2 ← Month No. of DATE 2
YY2 ← Year No. of DATE 2
Step 5. IF MM1 <= 2
THEN F1 ← YY1 – 1
G1 ← MM1 + 13
ELSE
F1 ← YY1
G1 ← MM1 + 1
END-IF
Step 6. IF MM2 <= 2
THEN F2 ← YY2 – 1
G2 ← MM2 + 13
ELSE
F2 ← YY2
G2 ← MM2 + 13
END-IF
Step 7. [COMPUTE N1] $N1 \leftarrow 1461 . \frac{F1}{4} + 153 . \frac{G1}{5} + DD$
Step 8. COMPUTE $N2 \leftarrow 1461 . \frac{F2}{4} + 153 . \frac{G2}{5} + DD$
Step 9. [CALCULATE THE NO. OF DAYS IN BETWEEN]
D ← N2 – N1
Step 10. PRINT D
Step 11. PRINT "WISH TO CONTINUE? (Y/N)"
Step 12. INPUT TO WISH
Step 13. END

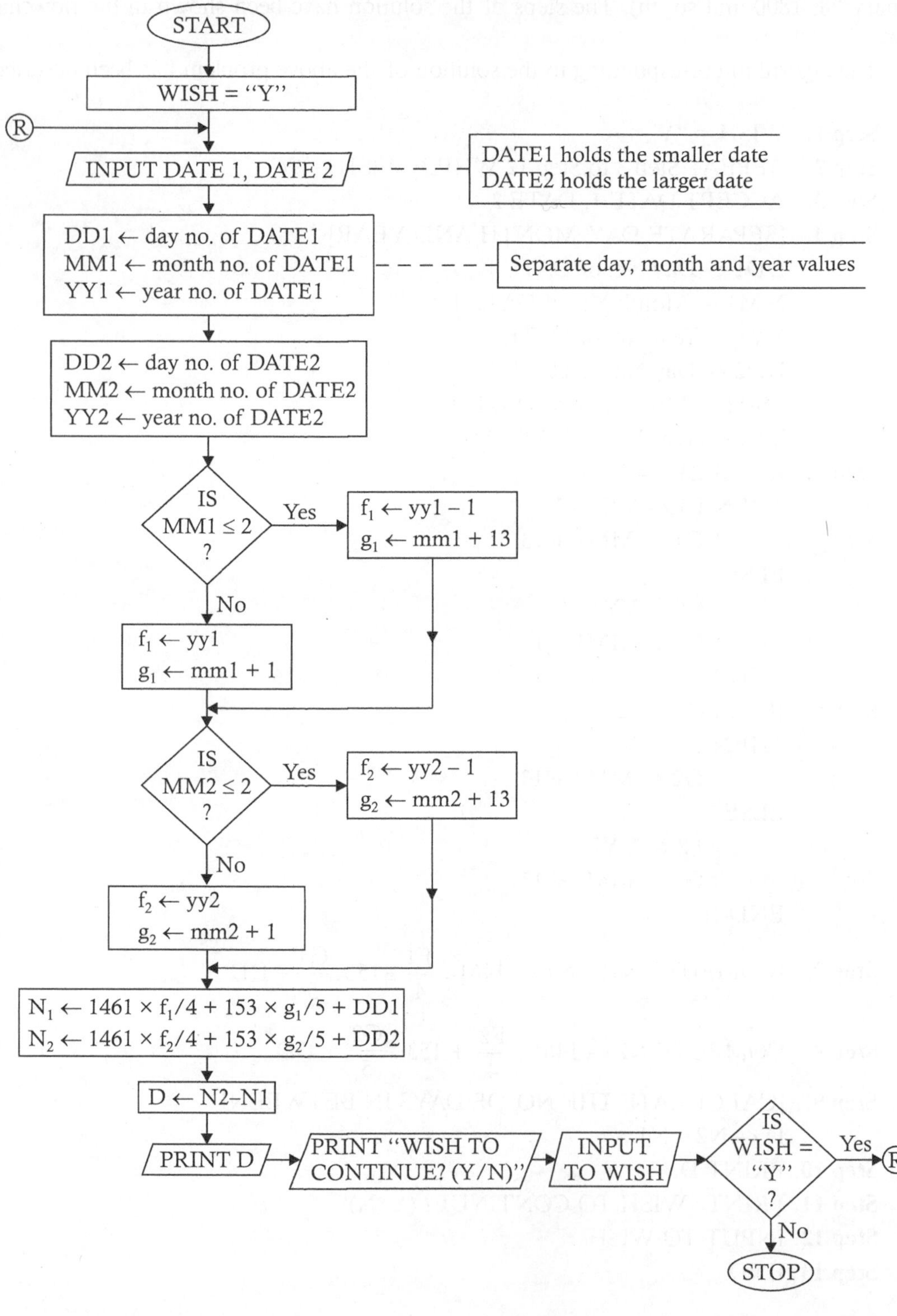
START
WISH = "Y"
R
INPUT DATE 1, DATE 2
DATE1 holds the smaller date
DATE2 holds the larger date
DD1 ← day no. of DATE1
MM1 ← month no. of DATE1
YY1 ← year no. of DATE1
Separate day, month and year values
DD2 ← day no. of DATE2
MM2 ← month no. of DATE2
YY2 ← year no. of DATE2
IS MM1 ≤ 2 ?
Yes
f1 ← yy1 – 1
g1 ← mm1 + 13
No
f1 ← yy1
g1 ← mm1 + 1
IS MM2 ≤ 2 ?
Yes
f2 ← yy2 – 1
g2 ← mm2 + 13
No
f2 ← yy2
g2 ← mm2 + 1
N1 ← 1461 × f1/4 + 153 × g1/5 + DD1
N2 ← 1461 × f2/4 + 153 × g2/5 + DD2
D ← N2–N1
PRINT D
PRINT "WISH TO CONTINUE? (Y/N)"
INPUT TO WISH
IS WISH = "Y" ?
Yes
R
No
STOP

Problem 3.42. *Construct a flowchart to show how to determine the name of the starting day of any given year.*

Task Analysis. The name of a year can be determined on the basis of a day-code that varies from 0 to 6. The day-code value 0 implies 'Sunday', day-code value 1 implies 'Monday' and so on. The day-code of a year X can be determined by the following formula :

$$\text{day-code} = \left[X + \left[\frac{x-1}{4}\right] - \left[\frac{x-1}{100}\right] + \left[\frac{x-1}{400}\right]\right] \text{mod } 7$$

where $[a]$ denotes the greatest integer less than or equal to a. For example [5.6] is 5. This is also known as floor value. Mod 7 implies remainder after division by 7.

The day-code value can also be computed by taking the value of N computed in the preceding problem and then subtracting 621,049 from it and then taking the result modulo 7. Here we shall use the previous procedure to construct the following flowchart because that holds good for any year.

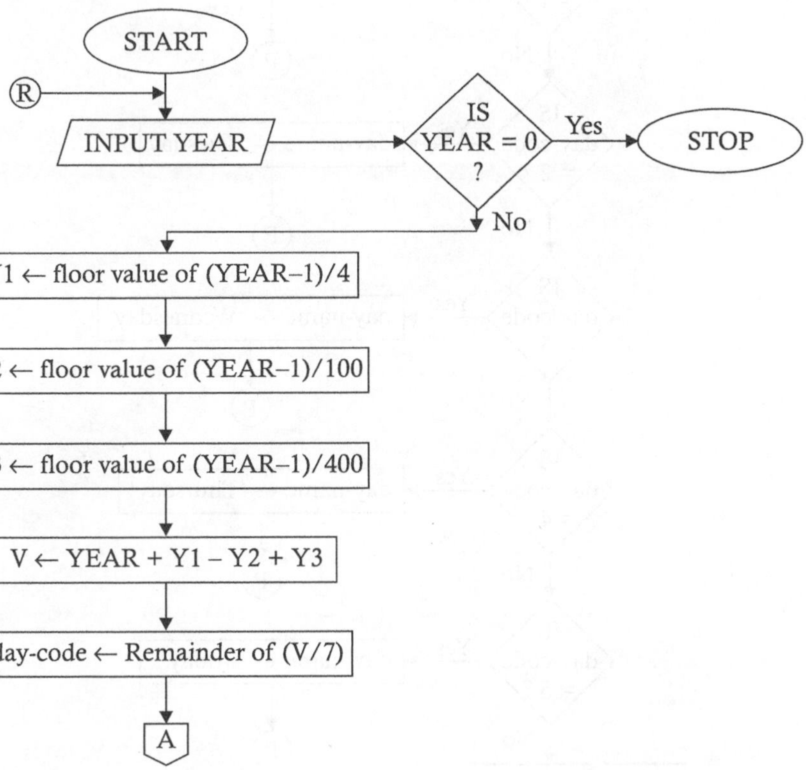

The algorithm corresponding to the solution of the above problem has been stated below :

Step 1. REPEAT step 2 through step 10

Step 2. ACCEPT YEAR as input

Step 3. IF YEAR = 0
THEN STOP
END-IF

Step 4. COMPUTE Y1 ← Floor value of (Year – 1)/4

Step 5. COMPUTE Y2 ← Floor value of (Year – 1)/100
Step 6. COMPUTE Y3 ← Floor value of (Year – 1)/400
Step 7. COMPUTE V ← YEAR + Y1 – Y2 + Y3

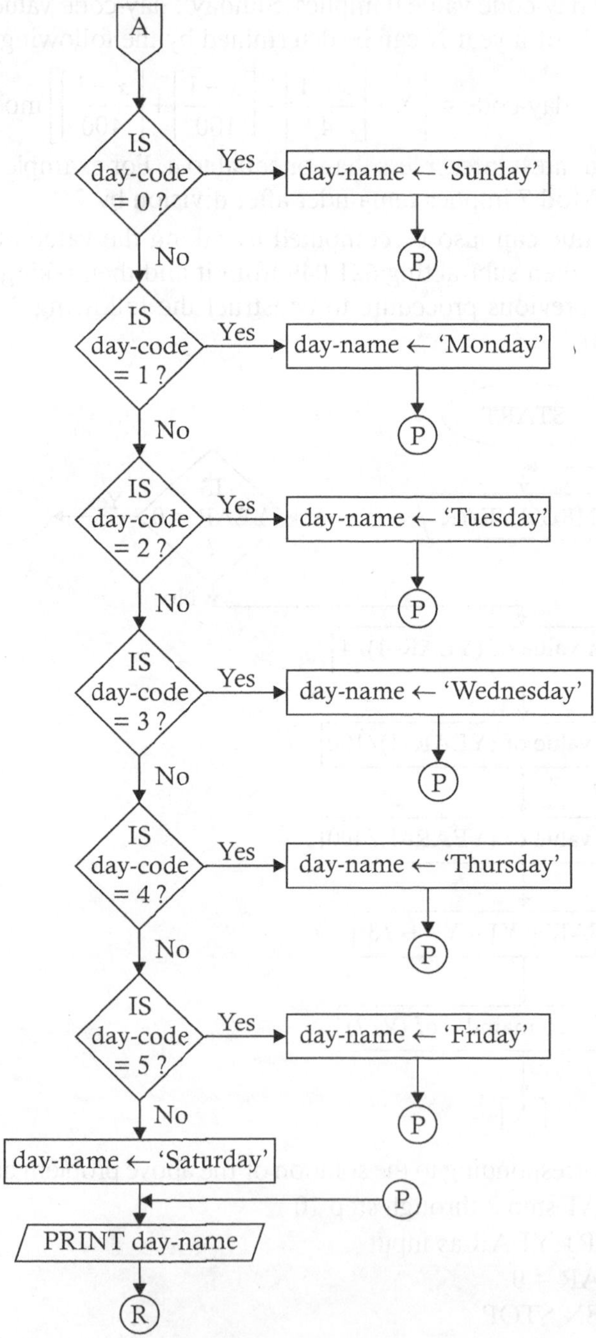

Step 8. COMPUTE DAY-CODE ← REMAINDER OF (V/7)

Step 9. IF DAY-CODE = 0

```
THEN DAY-NAME ← "SUNDAY"
ELSE
  IF DAY-CODE = 1
    THEN DAY-NAME ← "MONDAY"
    ELSE IF DAY-CODE = 2
    THEN DAY-NAME ← "TUESDAY"
  ELSE IF DAY-CODE = 3
      THEN  DAY-NAME ← "WEDNESDAY"
      ELSE IF DAY-CODE = 4
        THEN DAY-NAME ← "THURSDAY"
        ELSE IF DAY-CODE = 5
          THEN DAY-NAME ← "FRIDAY"
            ELSE IF DAY-CODE = 6
              THEN DAY-NAME ← "SATURDAY"
            END-IF
          END-IF
        END-IF
      END-IF
    END-IF
  END-IF
END-IF
```

Step 10. PRINT DAY-NAME

Step 11. STOP

EXERCISE 3

Construct flowcharts to show :

(*i*) How to print multiplication tables from 1 to 5.

(*ii*) Sum of the digits of a given number until it is reduced to a single digit.

(*iii*) A pyramid of numbers consisting of a given number of lines. For example, if the given no. is 5 then we shall see the following.

```
                1
            1   2   1
        1   2   3   2   1
    1   2   3   4   3   2   1
1   2   3   4   5   4   3   2   1
```

(*iv*) Sum of the digits of a given no.

(*v*) A menu of fruits as given below, accept the user's option. Calculate the cost of fruits and repeat the same until user's option is exit and finally display the cost of each item and the total amount to be paid by the customer.

Fruits Menu

	Fruits	**Cost per Kg. (in Rs.)**
1.	Mango	25.00
2.	Apple	45.00
3.	Grapes	55.00
4.	Exit	

(*vi*) The following patterns with flexible dimensions as supplied by the uses :

(*a*)

```
        ★
      ★ ★
    ★ ★ ★
  ★ ★ ★ ★
★ ★ ★ ★ ★
```

(*b*)

```
      ★
    ★ ★ ★
  ★ ★ ★ ★ ★
★ ★ ★ ★ ★ ★ ★
```

(*c*)

```
★ ★ ★ ★ ★ ★ ★
★ ★ ★ ★ ★ ★ ★
★ ★ ★ ★ ★ ★ ★
```

(*d*)

```
★ ★ ★ ★ ★ ★ ★ ★
★
★ ★ ★ ★ ★ ★ ★ ★
```

(*e*)

```
★ ★ ★ ★ ★
★ ★ ★ ★
★ ★ ★
★ ★
★
```

(*f*)

```
      ★
    ★ ★ ★
  ★ ★ ★ ★ ★
★ ★ ★ ★ ★ ★ ★
  ★ ★ ★ ★ ★
    ★ ★ ★
      ★
```

(*vii*) To read a six-digit positive integer. If the number is even, add up its digits else multiply the individual digits and print the result.

(*viii*) To obtain the decimal equivalent of a binary number.

(*ix*) To display all characters represented by the ASCII numbers from 25 to 100.

(*x*) To determine the value of an exponential expression of the form a^x, where a is any number and x is any integer.

(*xi*) To determine the HCF of n given numbers.

(*xii*) To determine the maximum and the minimum ones of n given numbers.

(*xiii*) To determine all the permutations of the numbers less than or equal to some given number n. For example, if n = 123, then the permutations are :

123
321
231
132
213
312

(*xiv*) To find out a series of five consecutive numbers, the sum of the squares of the first three of which is equal to the sum of the squares of the last two. For example,

$$(-2)^2 + (-1)^2 + 0^2 = 1^2 + 2^2$$

(*xv*) Limit the checking within 1000, to show all the triad numbers within 10,000. A number is said to be a triad number if the double and triple of the number contain all separate digits with no repetition of any one of them.

(*xvi*) To identify and show the integer values of x, y and z that satisfy the equation : $Z^2 = X^2 + y^2$.

4 PROBLEMS ON ARRAYS

INTRODUCTION

Think of a road with a row of houses. What is common to all houses ? The answer is the name of the road on which a house is situated. How would you get a unique address of a house on the road ? It is by taking the name of the road and the house number of the lot. An array is similar to a road with a number of houses. The name of the road can be thought of as the name of the array and the number of the house can be thought of as the location number of the array.

Formally speaking, an array is a finite collection of homogeneous data values usually stored in consecutive memory locations having a common name. The term *finite* implies that the number of data values of an array must be limited by its size. The term *homogeneous* means 'having same nature or characteristic'. The term *usually* implies that arrays are almost always implemented by using contiguous locations of computer's main memory in a linearly ordered fashion, but not always. The common name assigned to a set of adjacent memory locations to hold data of a particular type is called the name of the array. The different data values of an array are mentioned by using the name of the array along with a subscript within brackets, such as, A[1], A(1), A[2] etc. or in general A[i], where i must be an integer. The value of i indicates the location being mentioned. The subscript is also called an index. This is why an array element such as A[i] is also called an indexed or subscripted variable. Following are some examples of arrays :

1. The roll numbers of the students of a class stored in computer's main memory in a linear order.
2. The names of the students of a class stored in computer's main memory in a linear order.
3. The maximum temperatures of different days of a month in a city stored in computer's memory in a linear order.

In each of the above cases the type of all the data stored together is identical *i.e.,* homogeneous. For example, the roll numbers are usually integers, the names are usually strings of characters and the temperatures are usually fractional or floating point numbers. Hence the first example is an array of integers, the second example is an array of strings and the third example is an array of floating point numbers. Different computer languages use different notations to represent the array elements. However, we will stick to a particular notation. If A is an array of size n, then we will point to an array element by the notation $A(i)$ where the value of i can vary from 1 to n.

Problem 4.1. *Our first target is to show you how to construct an array. The following algorithm will clarify the steps :*

1. Decide the size of the array to be formed, say n.
2. Declare an array of size n with some desired name, say A.
3. Initialize the variable or location that will be used as a subscript, say i, with a statement like $i \leftarrow 1$.
4. Repeat steps 5 and 6 until $i > n$.
5. Accept the data value for the array element $A(i)$.
6. Increment the value of the subscript : $i \leftarrow i + 1$.
7. Stop.

In most of the programming languages the first two steps can be performed in a single statement where the size n is predefined, such as int A[100] defines an array of integers of size 100.

The following flowchart depicts the above algorithm.

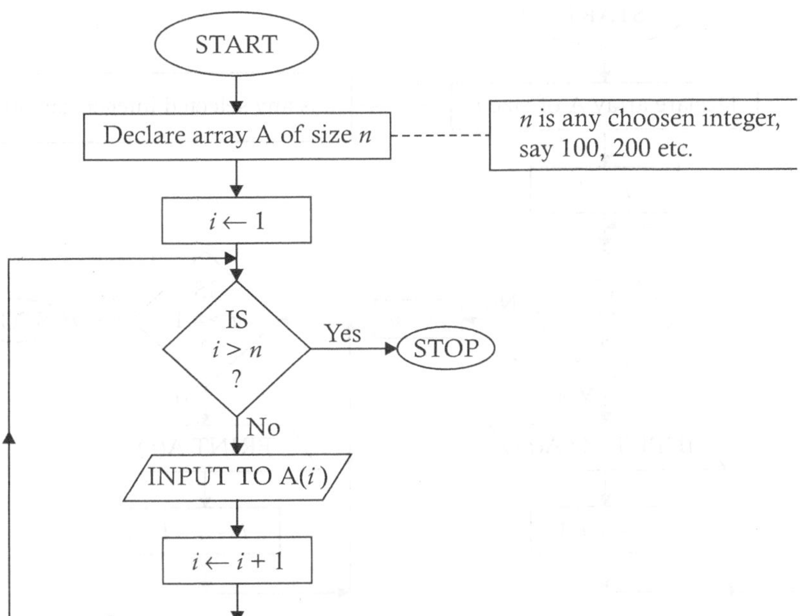

However, mere construction of an array will not fulfill any useful purpose of a person. The stored values of an array are to be manipulated to achieve some target of the user; otherwise, the labour of creating the array will go in vain. The manipulation may be simple viewing of the data stored or it may comprise some arithmetic or logical operations on the stored data.

The algorithm corresponding to the above problem is given below :

Step 1. Declare the array A(1 ... N) of N elements to be reversed.

Step 2. Repeat step 3 for I = 1 to N

Step 3. Accept a data value at the Ith location.

Step 4. Set I = 0, J = N + 1

Step 5. Repeat steps 6 through 7 Until I >= J

Step 6. I ← I + 1, J = J – 1

Step 7. T ← A (I)
A(I) ← A(J)
A(J) ← T

Step 8. Repeat step 9 for I = 1 to N

Step 9. PRINT A(I)

Step 10. STOP

Problem 4.4. *Construct a flowchart to show how to determine the maximum number in a set of n numbers.*

Task Analysis. The maximum number in a set of numbers is that number which is greater than or equal to all other numbers in the set. The maximum number may not be unique and it is only defined for sets of one or more elements. The simplest and most systematic way to find out the desired number is achieved if we consider the first number as our temporary candidate for the maximum and write it in a separate place, say MAX and then we scan the list from the 2nd number through the last number of the list to find out any number which is greater than the number stored in MAX. If we face such a number, we store it in MAX by removing the previously stored one. At the end of the scanning process, we can declare that MAX contains the largest number in the given set. The algorithm of the solution is given here.

Step 1. Accept the size of the set, n

Step 2. Declare an array A(1 ... n) of n elements where $n \geq 1$

Step 3. Repeat step 4 for I = 1, 2, ..., n

Step 4. Accept a number to A(I)

Step 5. [Set temporary maximum MAX to first array element] MAX ← A(1)

Step 6. Repeat step 7 for I = 2, 3, ..., n

Step 7. If A(I) > MAX,
Then MAX ← A(I)
End-if

Step 8. Print MAX as the maximum for the array of n elements

Step 9. Stop.

The flowchart showing the logic of the above solution is shown below :

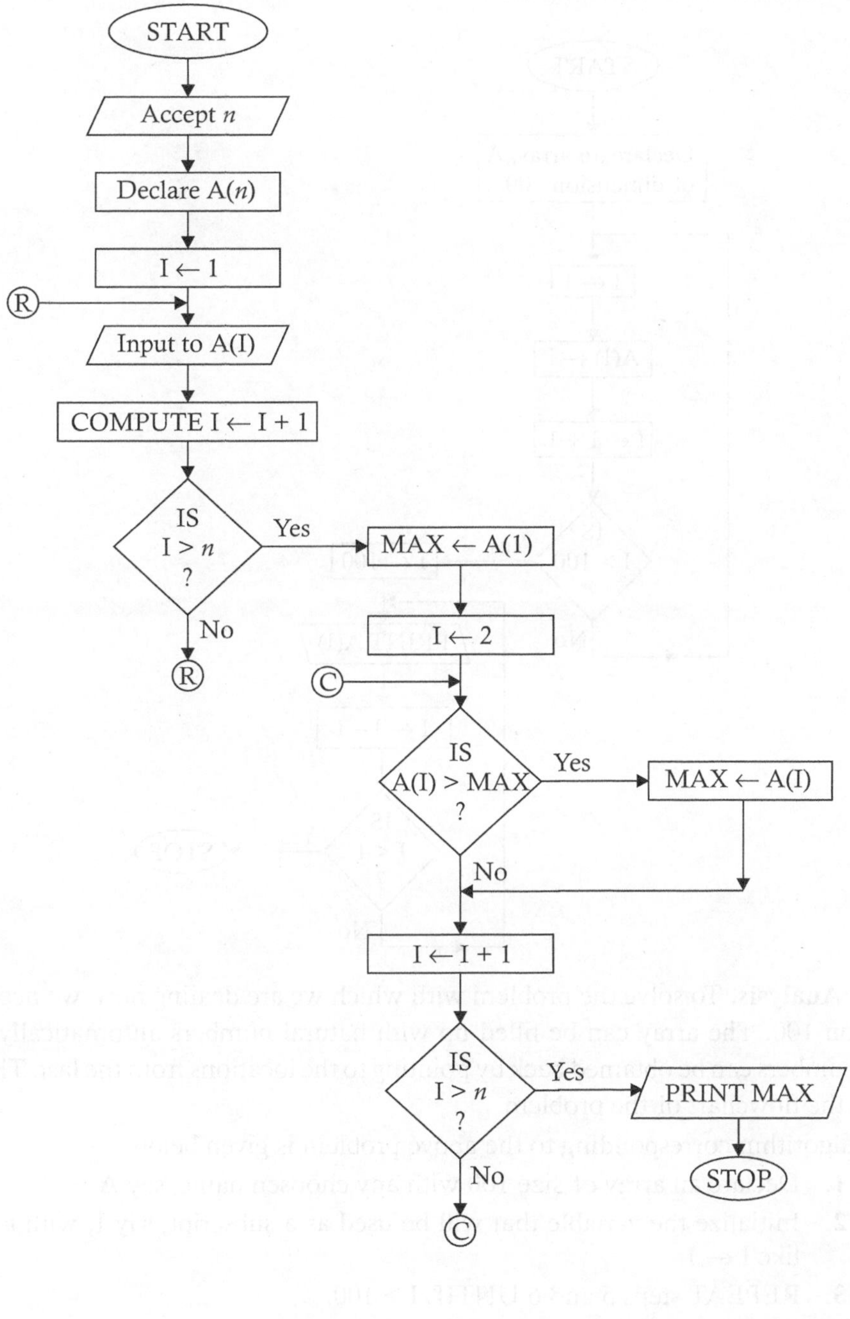

Problem 4.5. *Construct a flowchart to show how to store the first 100 natural numbers in an array and then to show them back in the reverse sequence.*

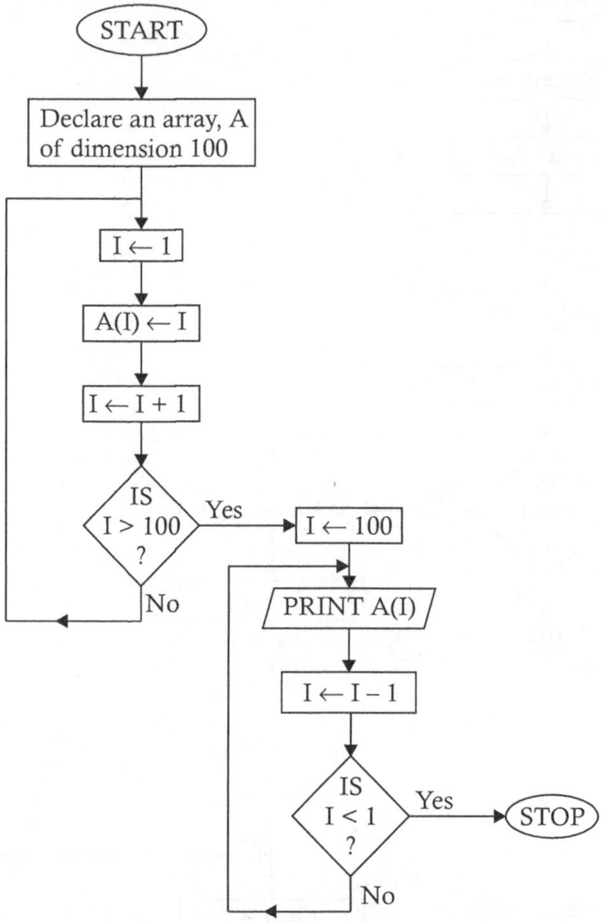

Task Analysis. To solve the problem with which we are dealing now, we need an array of dimension 100. The array can be filled up with natural numbers automatically and once stored, the numbers can be obtained back by pointing to the locations from the last. The solution is shown in the flowchart of the problem.

The algorithm corresponding to the above problem is given below :

Step 1. Declare an array of size 100 with any choosen name, say A.

Step 2. Initialize the variable that will be used as a subscript, say I, with a statement like I ← 1

Step 3. REPEAT steps 5 and 6 UNTIL I > 100.

Step 4. A(I) ← I

Step 5. I ← I + 1

Step 6. Initialize I again with the starting print location, I ← 100

Step 7. REPEAT STEPS 9 & 10 UNTIL I < 1

Step 8. PRINT A(I)

Step 9. I ← I – 1

Step 10. END

Problem 4.6. *In a certain hospital, the weights of newborn babies are recorded over each month and then processed at the end of the month to determine the following :*

(i) Mean weight of the babies

(ii) Maximum of the weights and

(iii) Minimum of the weights.

Construct a flowchart to show how the weights can be stored in the computer's memory first and then processed to determine the desired outputs.

Task Analysis. Here the solution is to include the procedure of storing the weights of the babies first. This will require an array. Let us suppose that the dimension of the array can be given as input during the execution of the procedure, so that the array can be defined during the execution (If it is not possible then an array of size 100 may be defined and then the requisite number of locations can be used). The next task is to determine the maximum of the weights recorded. For this purpose, we assume that the weight stored in the first location is the maximum one and hence we store its value to some location, say MAX. Next, we compare the values of the remaining locations one by one with the value of the MAX ; if it happens that some location contains a weight greater than that of the MAX, then we store that weight in MAX by removing the previous one so that at the end of the comparison, the location MAX will contain the maximum of the weights. Similarly, the minimum of the weights can be determined by defining a location, say MIN, with the initial value of the first location and then comparing the value of MIN with the values of the remaining locations to find out the value lesser then the value contained in MIN. The procedures are shown in the flowchart below :

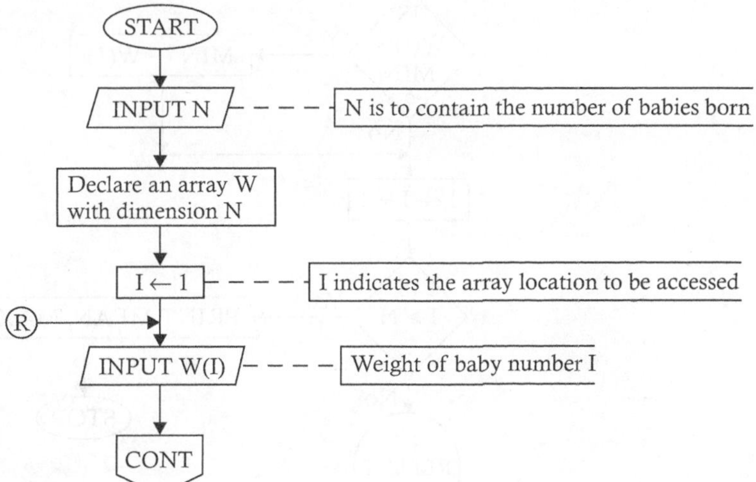

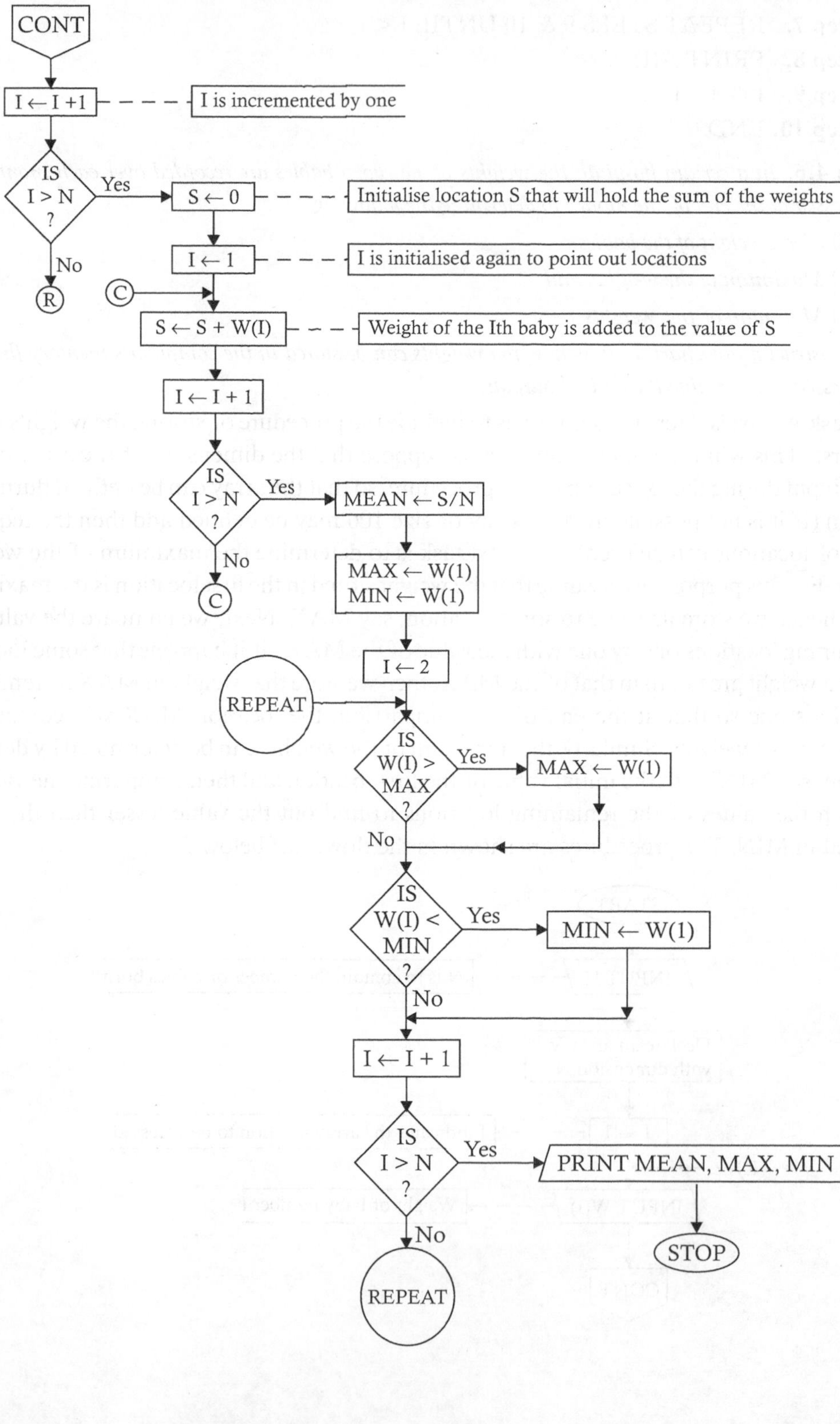
CONT
I ← I +1
I is incremented by one
IS I > N ?
Yes
No
R
S ← 0
Initialise location S that will hold the sum of the weights
I ← 1
I is initialised again to point out locations
C
S ← S + W(I)
Weight of the Ith baby is added to the value of S
I ← I + 1
IS I > N ?
Yes
No
C
MEAN ← S/N
MAX ← W(1)
MIN ← W(1)
I ← 2
REPEAT
IS W(I) > MAX ?
Yes
No
MAX ← W(1)
IS W(I) < MIN ?
Yes
No
MIN ← W(1)
I ← I + 1
IS I > N ?
Yes
No
PRINT MEAN, MAX, MIN
STOP
REPEAT

The algorithm corresponding to the above problem is given below :

Step 1. ACCEPT THE SIZE(N) OF THE ARRAY AS INPUT
Step 2. DECLARE AN ARRAY W OF SIZE N.
Step 3. I ← 1 [INITIALIZE THE VARIABLE I WITH 1 FOR USE AS A SUBSCRIPT]
Step 4. REPEAT STEPS 5 and 6 WHILE I < = N
Step 5. INPUT TO W(I) [W(I) is to hold the weight of Ith baby given as input]
Step 6. COMPUTE I ← I + 1 [INCREMENT I]
Step 7. S ← 0 [INITIALIZE S which is to hold the sum of the weights of the babies]
Step 8. I ← 1
Step 9. REPEAT STEPS 10 and 11 WHILE I <= N
Step 10. COMPUTE S ← S + W(I)
Step 11. COMPUTE I ← I + 1
Step 12. COMPUTE MEAN ← $\frac{S}{N}$
Step 13. MAX ← W(1) [Initialize MAX with the weight of the 1st baby]
Step 14. MIN ← W(1) [Initialize MIN with the weight of the 1st baby]
Step 15. I ← 2 [Set I to 2, to start comparison with the weight of the 2nd baby onwards]
Step 16. REPEAT STEPS 17 THROUGH 19 WHILE I <= N
Step 17. IF W(I) > MAX
THEN MAX ← W(I)
END-IF
Step 18. IF W(I) < MIN
THEN MIN ← W(I)
END-IF
Step 19. COMPUTE I ← I + 1
Step 20. PRINT MEAN, MAX, MIN
Step 21. STOP.

Problem 4.7. *In a certain city the maximum and the minimum temperatures on each day are recorded over each month to determine the following at the end of the month :*

(*i*) *Mean maximum temperature in the month*
(*ii*) *Mean minimum temperature in the month*
(*iii*) *Highest maximum temperature*
(*iv*) *Lowest minimum temperature*
(*v*) *Hottest day number of the month*
(*vi*) *Coldest day number of the month*

Draw a flowchart to show how the desired result can be obtained.

Task Analysis. This problem is similar to the preceding one. Hence the solution will also be similar. Here two arrays are required to store two types of data (maximum and minimum).

Step 5. REPEAT FOR I = 1, 2, 3, ..., N
(*a*) COMPUTE S1 ← S1 + MAX (I)
(*b*) COMPUTE S2 ← S2 + MIN(I)

Step 6. COMPUTE MAX-MEAN ← $\frac{S1}{N}$

Step 7. COMPUTE MIN-MEAN ← $\frac{S2}{N}$

Step 8. MAX-MAX ← MAX (1) [Initialize with the 1st temperature of the set]

Step 9. MIN-MIN ← MIN (1) [Initialize with the 1st temperature of the minimum set]

Step 10. HOTTEST ← 1, COLDEST ← 1
[Initialize with the 1st day number]

Step 11. REPEAT FOR I = 2, 3, 4, ..., N

```
    IF MAX (I) > MAX-MAX
        THEN MAX-MAX ← MAX (I)
             HOTTEST ← I
    END-IF
    IF MIN (I) < MIN-MIN
        THEN MIN-MIN ← MIN (I)
             COLDEST ← I
    END-IF
```

Step 12. PRINT MAX-MEAN, MIN-MEAN, MAX-MAX, MIN-MIN, HOTTEST, COLDEST

Step 13. END

Problem 4.8. *In an Institution three tests are held each out of 50. The better score between the first two is added to that of the third one to determine the final score and a grade is assigned to each student on the percentage score as per the following rules.*

Percentage in Score	*Grade*
> = 80	*S*
> = 70 but <80	*A*
> = 60 but <70	*B*
> = 50 but <60	*C*
< 50	*F*

Develop a flowchart to show how to accept the input data related to each student and process them to print out a result sheet with output in descending order of percentage score.

Task Analysis. Here the inputs are marks obtained by students in three tests. To indentify the student, the student roll-number and name of each student can also be given as input. Now, the final score of each student can be obtained by determining the greater score between those of the first two tests and then adding it to that of the third test. The total score will represent the percentage score because the total is based on the marks of two tests each of which carries a maximum mark of 50.

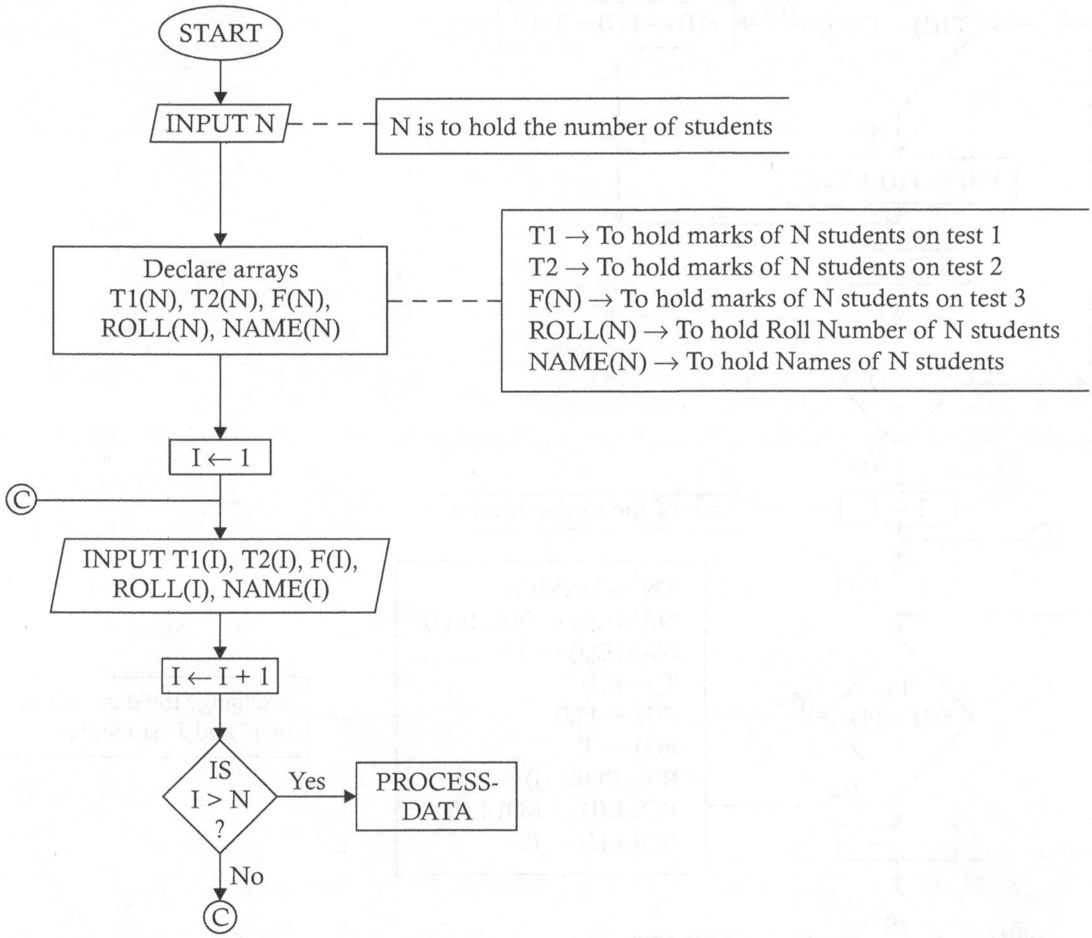

At this stage we shall have Roll Number, Name and Percentage of all the students. The next task is to sort the facts to get information about the students in descending seqence of percentage. To sort the facts, we take the percentage of the first student and compare it with the percentage of all other remaining students and interchange the student's data whenever some student's percentage is found to be less than the percentage of that of the first student's percentage. Similarly, we take the percentage of the second student to compare it with the percentage of the third student to the last student to interchange the facts if some student's percentage is found to be less than that of the second student. This type of comparison is continued until we compare the percentage of the last two students.

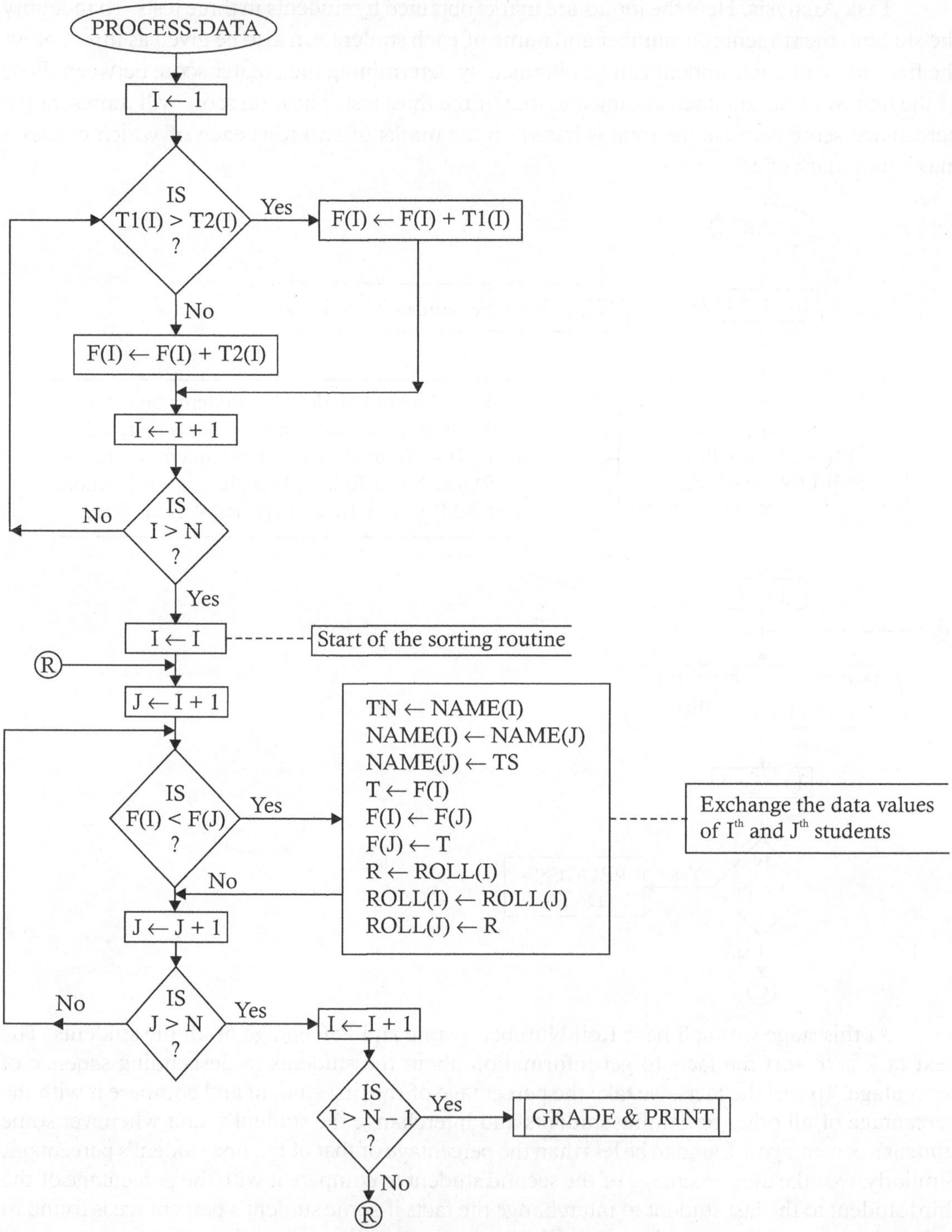
PROCESS-DATA
I ← 1
IS
T1(I) > T2(I)
?
Yes
F(I) ← F(I) + T1(I)
No
F(I) ← F(I) + T2(I)
I ← I + 1
IS
I > N
?
No
Yes
I ← I
Start of the sorting routine
R
J ← I + 1
IS
F(I) < F(J)
?
Yes
No
TN ← NAME(I)
NAME(I) ← NAME(J)
NAME(J) ← TS
T ← F(I)
F(I) ← F(J)
F(J) ← T
R ← ROLL(I)
ROLL(I) ← ROLL(J)
ROLL(J) ← R
Exchange the data values of Ith and Jth students
J ← J + 1
IS
J > N
?
No
Yes
I ← I + 1
IS
I > N – 1
?
Yes
GRADE & PRINT
No
R

During the interchange operations, the roll-number and the name of the students must also be interchanged. The procedure is illustrated in the flowchart given on previous page.

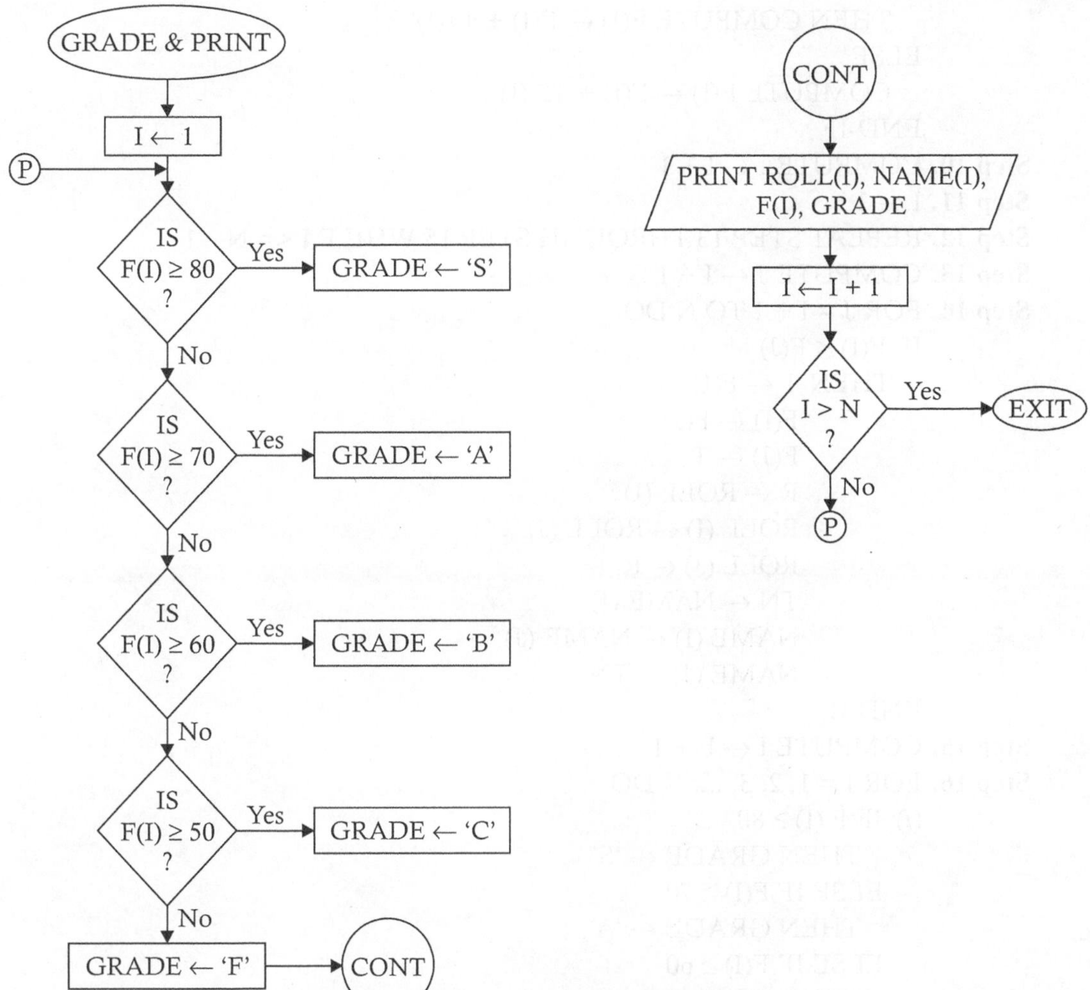

The algorithm of the above solution has been stated below :

Step 1. ACCEPT THE NUMBER OF STUDENTS N

Step 2. DECLARE FIVE ARRAYS, NAMELY, T1(I), T2(I), F(I), ROLL (I) & NAME (I) RESPECTIVELY TO HOLD SCORE OF TEST 1, TEST 2, TEST 3, ROLL NUMBER & NAME OF THE STUDENTS.

Step 3. I ← 1 [INITIALIZE I]

Step 4. REPEAT STEP 5 THROUGH STEP 6 WHILE I <= N

Step 5. INPUT TO T1(I), T2(I), F(I), ROLL (I), NAME (I)

Step 6. COMPUTE I ← I + 1

```
Step 7.  I ← I
Step 8.  DO STEP 9 and STEP 10 WHILE I <= N
Step 9.  IF T1 (I) > T2 (I)
           THEN COMPUTE F(I) ← F(I) + T1(I)
         ELSE
           COMPUTE F(I) ← F(I) + T2 (I)
         END-IF
Step 10. COMPUTE I ← I + 1
Step 11. I ← 1
Step 12. REPEAT STEP 13 THROUGH STEP 15 WHILE I <= N – 1
Step 13. COMPUTE J ← I + 1
Step 14. FOR J = I + 1 TO N DO
         IF F(I) < F(J)
           THEN T ← F(I)
                F(I) ← F(J)
                F(J) ← T
                R ← ROLL (I)
                ROLL (I) ← ROLL (J)
                ROLL (J) ← R
                TN ← NAME (I)
                NAME (I) ← NAME (J)
                NAME (J) ← TN
         END-IF
Step 15. COMPUTE I ← I  + 1
Step 16. FOR I = 1, 2, 3, ..., N DO
         (i) IF F (I) ≥ 80
               THEN GRADE ← 'S'
             ELSE IF F(I) ≥ 70
               THEN GRADE ← 'A'
             ELSE IF F(I) ≥ 60
               THEN GRADE ← 'B'
             ELSE IF F(I) ≥ 50
               THEN GRADE ← 'C'
             ELSE
               GRADE ← 'F'
             END-IF
             END-IF
             END-IF
             END-IF
         (ii) PRINT F(I), ROLL (I), NAME (I), GRADE
Step 17. STOP
```

Problem 4.9. *Construct a flowchart to show how a set of N numbers is stored in memory and then stored in ascending order of their magnitude for display.*

Task Analysis. Let us suppose that the list of numbers A(1), A(2), ..., A(N) is in memory. We shall use the bubble sort algorithm that works as follows:

Step 1. We compare A(1) and A(2) and arrange them in the desired order, so that A(1) < A(2). We next compare A(2) and A(3) so that A(2) < A(3). We continue this way until we compare A(N – 1) with A(N) and arrange them so that A(N – 1) < A(N). These comparisons bubbles up the largest element to the Nth position *i.e.,* the largest of the elements comes in A(N) after these N – 1 comparisons.

Step 2. As the largest element has been placed properly in step 1, we need not disturb the A(N) element. So we repeat the comparisons in step 1 without A(N). This will bubble up the second largest element in A(N – 1).

We repeat these comparisons each time considering one less element than that in the preceding step. It can be observed that after (N – 1) steps, the set of numbers will be in sorted sequence. The following flowchart shows the procedure :

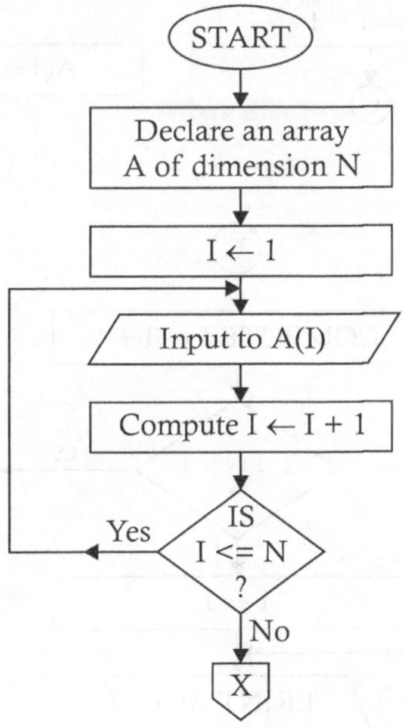

The algorithm of the above process is stated below :

Step 1. FOR I = 1 TO N

Step 2. INPUT TO A(I)

Step 3. END-FOR

Step 4. FOR I = 1 TO N – 1

Step 5. FOR J = 1 TO N – I

Step 6. IF A(J) > A(J + 1)

THEN T ← A(J)

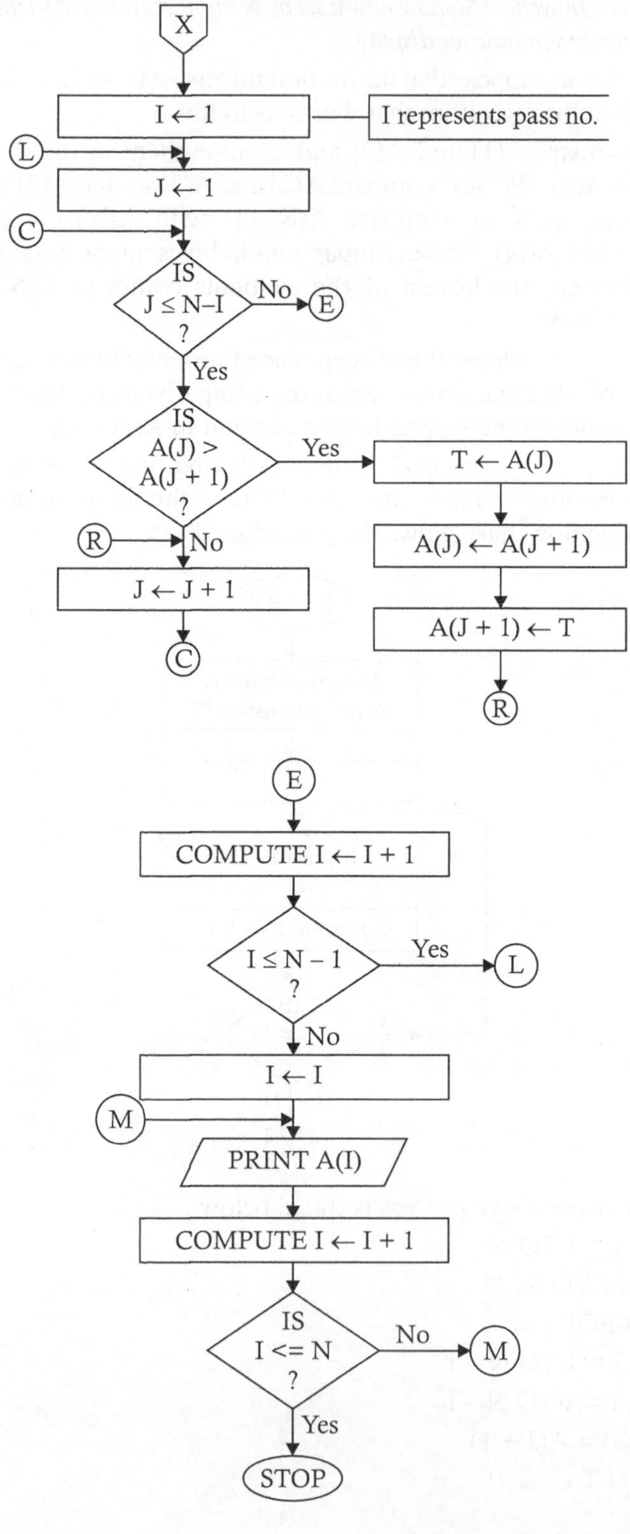
X
I ← 1
I represents pass no.
L
J ← 1
C
IS
J ≤ N–I
?
No
E
Yes
IS
A(J) >
A(J + 1)
?
Yes
T ← A(J)
A(J) ← A(J + 1)
A(J + 1) ← T
R
No
J ← J + 1
C
R
E
COMPUTE I ← I + 1
I ≤ N – 1
?
Yes
L
No
I ← I
M
PRINT A(I)
COMPUTE I ← I + 1
IS
I <= N
?
No
M
Yes
STOP

A(J) ← A(J + 1)

A(J + 1) ← T

END-IF

Step 7. END-FOR–J

Step 8. END-FOR–I

Step 9. FOR I = 1 TO N

Step 10. PRINT A(I)

Step 11. END-FOR–I

Step 12. STOP

Problem 4.10. *Draw a flowchart to show how the product of two matrices can be obtained.*

Task Analysis. We know that a matrix is a two dimensional array. The multiplication of two matrices will be possible if the number of columns of the first matrix is equal to the number of rows in the second matrix or if the number of rows in the first matrix equals the number of columns of the second matrix. Now if we consider the row by column multiplication of the two matrices then the elements of a row is taken one by one to multiply with the corresponding column elements taking one at a time and the sum of these products is taken as an element of the resulting matrix. This is repeated for all the rows of the first matrix. The reverse process is carried out for the column by row multiplication. To describe the process mathematically, let A = $[a_{ij}]$ be an $m \times n$ matrix and B = $[b_{ij}]$ be an $n \times p$ matrix. Then the product A.B of these matrices is of the order $m \times p$ say, C = $[c_{ij}]$.

where $c_{ij} = a_{i1} . b_{1j} + a_{i2} . b_{2j} + ... + a_{in} . b_{nj}$

$$\Rightarrow \qquad c_{ij} = \sum_{k=1}^{n} a_{ik} . b_{kj}$$

The procedure is shown in the flowchart below :

The algorithm of the above problem is given below :

Step 1. FOR I = 1 TO 5

Step 2. FOR J = 1 TO 5

Step 3. Input TO M1(I, J), M2 (I, J)

Step 4. NEXT J

Step 5. NEXT I

Step 6. FOR I = 1 TO 5

Step 7. FOR J = 1 TO 5

Step 8. M3 (I, J) = 0

Step 9. FOR K = 1 TO 5

Step 10. COMPUTE M3 (I, J) ← M3(I, J) + M1(I, K) * M2(K, J)

Step 11. END-FOR-K

Step 12. END-FOR-J

Step 13. END-FOR-I

Step 14. FOR I = 1 TO 5

Step 15. FOR J = 1 TO 5

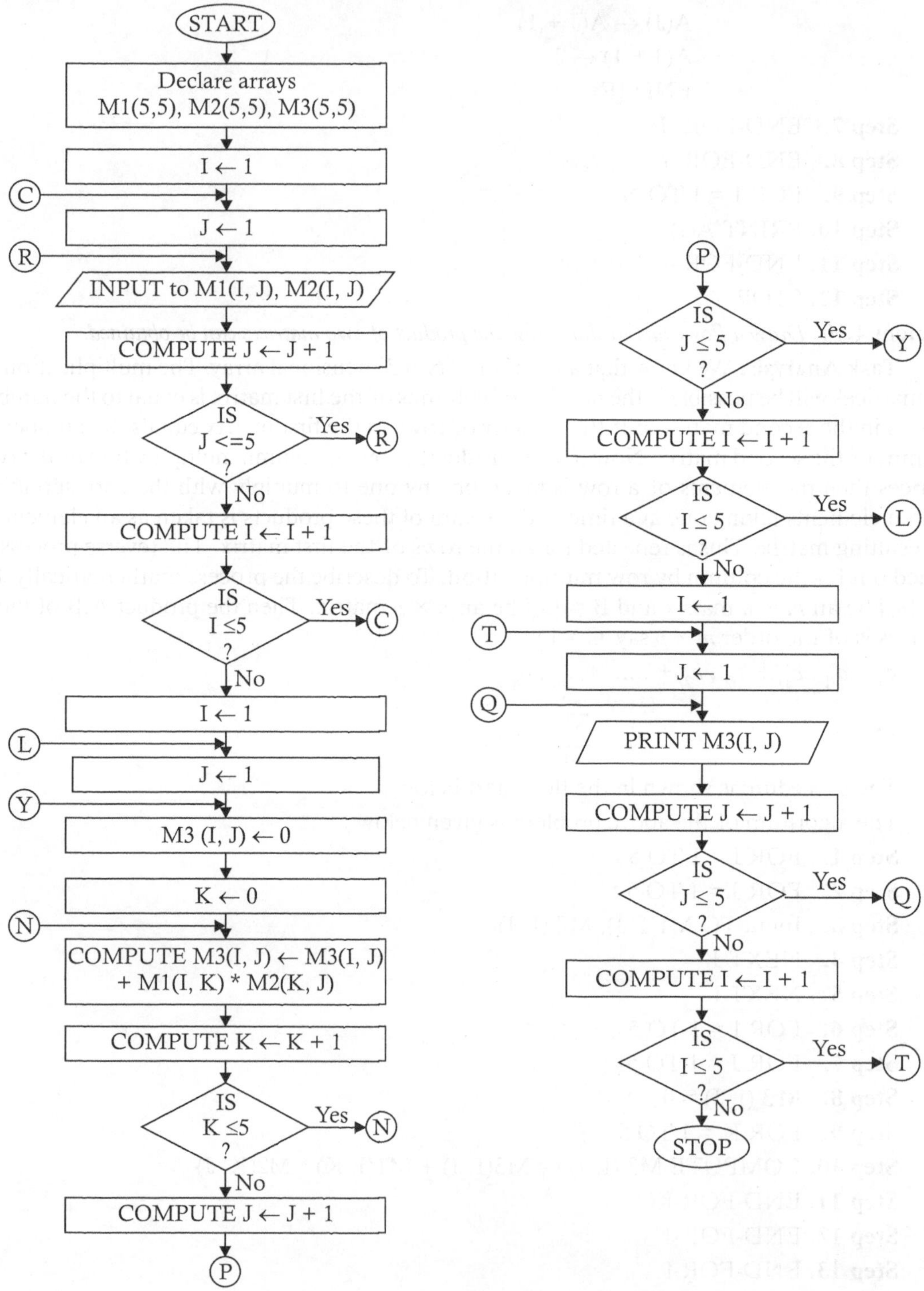
START
Declare arrays
M1(5,5), M2(5,5), M3(5,5)
I ← 1
C
J ← 1
R
INPUT to M1(I, J), M2(I, J)
COMPUTE J ← J + 1
IS
J <=5
?
Yes
R
No
COMPUTE I ← I + 1
IS
I ≤5
?
Yes
C
No
I ← 1
L
J ← 1
Y
M3 (I, J) ← 0
K ← 0
N
COMPUTE M3(I, J) ← M3(I, J)
+ M1(I, K) * M2(K, J)
COMPUTE K ← K + 1
IS
K ≤5
?
Yes
N
No
COMPUTE J ← J + 1
P
P
IS
J ≤ 5
?
Yes
Y
No
COMPUTE I ← I + 1
IS
I ≤ 5
?
Yes
L
No
I ← 1
T
J ← 1
Q
PRINT M3(I, J)
COMPUTE J ← J + 1
IS
J ≤ 5
?
Yes
Q
No
COMPUTE I ← I + 1
IS
I ≤ 5
?
Yes
T
No
STOP

Step 16. PRINT M3 (I, J)
Step 17. END-FOR-J
Step 18. END-FOR-I
Step 19. STOP

Problem 4.11. *A departmental store-chain consists of 15 stores, each comprising 7 departments. The weekly sales-totals of each department of the stores are available for processing.*

Develop a flowchart to show how the data are to be processed to determine total Weekly Sales.
(i) Departmentwise and (ii) Storewise.

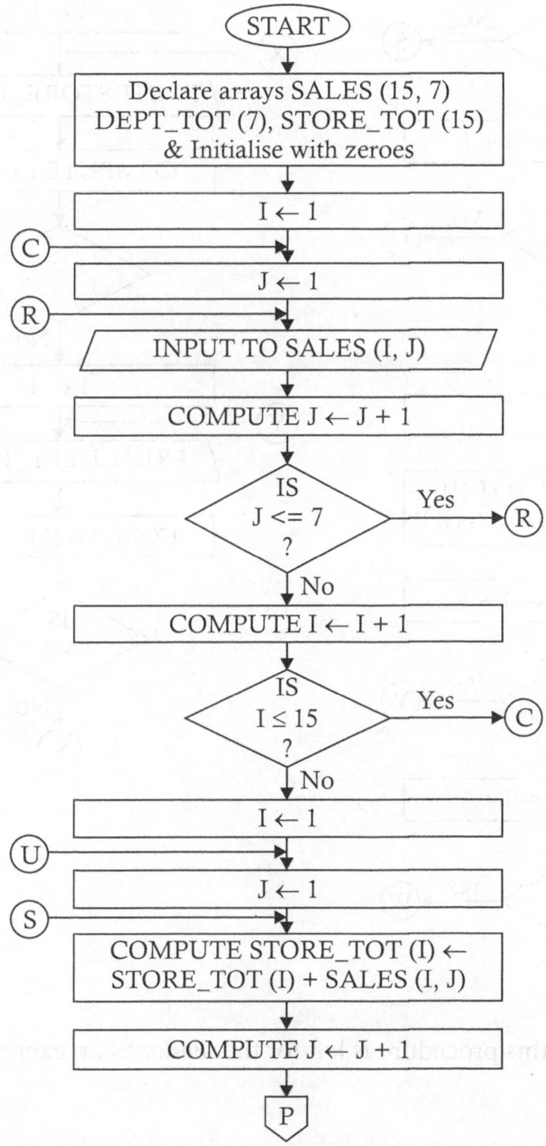

Task Analysis. Here we need three arrays : One two-dimensional array to hold the sales-values ; two one dimensional arrays, one to hold departmentwise totals and the other to hold storewise averages. The procedure involves row-wise addition of 2D array-values when the total for each store is determined and column-wise addition of the 2D array-values when the total for each department is determined. The following flowchart is meant to show the process.

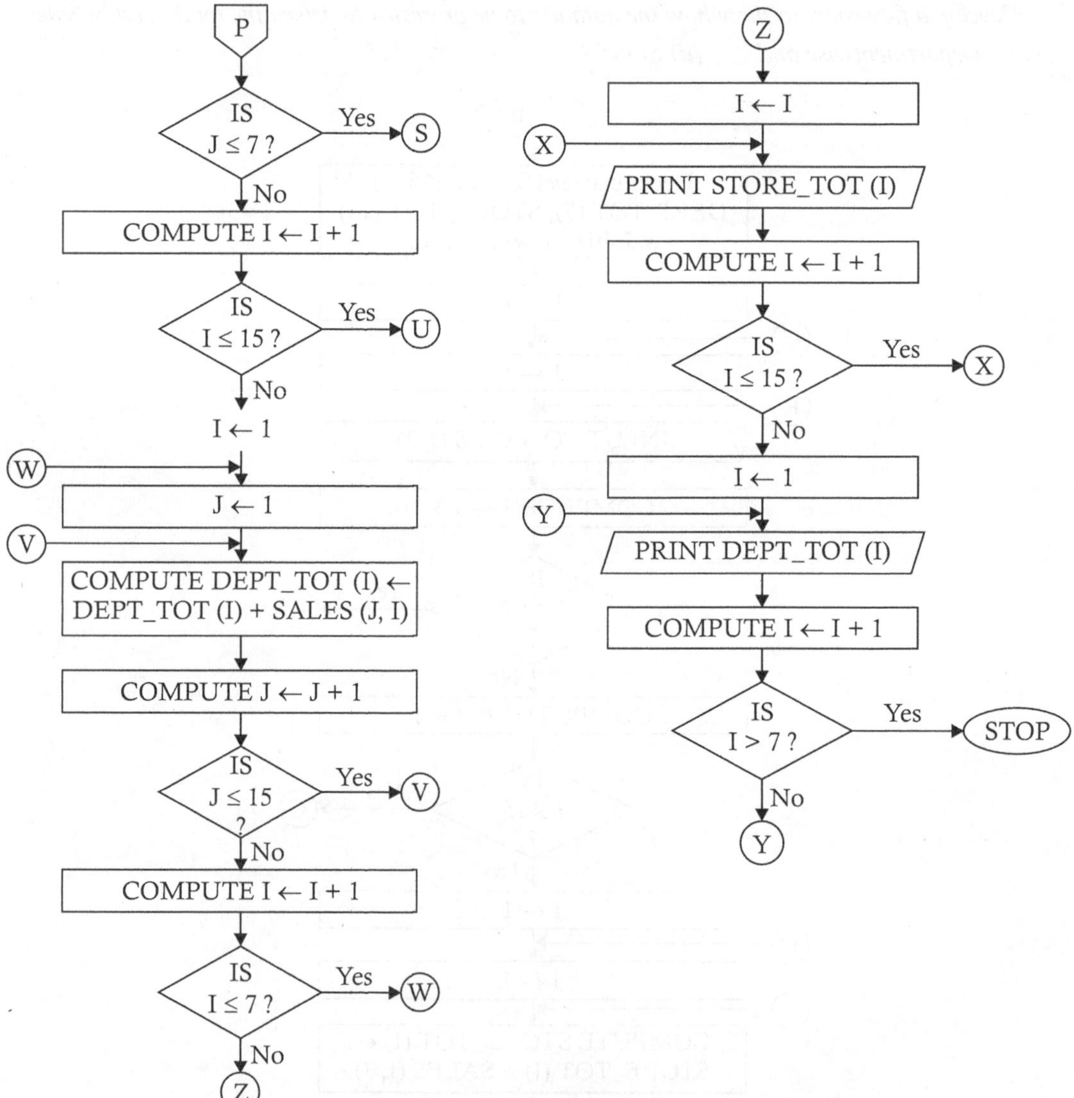

The algorithm of this procedure is left for the reader as an exercise.

EXERCISE 4

Construct flowcharts and algorithms for the following problems :

4.1. To convert a decimal number into its equivalent binary, octal or hexadecimal form according to given option.

4.2. To test whether a given string is a palindrome or not.

4.3. To count number of vowels, consonents, and special characters in a given string.

4.4. To unscramble a four letter word

[**Hint.** Let abcd be the given four-character string ; then the process should find out all the words by jumbling the characters, such as acbd, adbc ...... etc.]

4.5. To convert a given Roman numeral into its decimal equivalent. The following table gives the Roman symbols and their decimal equivalents :

Roman	Decimal
M	1000
D	500
C	100
L	50
X	10
V	5
I	1

The algorithm for converting a Roman numeral

R1 R2 ......R*n*

to decimal is given below :

1. I ← 1
   (I denotes the position of the symbol being scanned)
2. DECIMAL ← 0
   DECIMAL is to hold the decimal value of the given Roman numeral)
3. REPEAT steps 4 through 6 WHILE I < N.
4. If the decimal value of R_i is greater than or equal to the decimal value of R_{i+1}, add the decimal value of R_i to DECIMAL else subtract the decimal value of R_i from DECIMAL.
5. COMPUTE I ← I + 1.
6. END-WHILE.
7. ADD the decimal value of R_n to DECIMAL.
8. PRINT DECIMAL.
9. STOP.

4.6. To convert a decimal numeral into its Roman equivalent.

4.7. To show that Goldback's conjecture in mathematics is true for all the positive even numbers within 500.

(Goldback stated that every even integer greater than 2 can be expressed as the sum of two prime numbers)

4.8. The maximum and the minimum temperatures on each day of a city are collected over each month and then processed to determine (*i*) Average minimum temperature of the month.

(*ii*) Average maximum temperature of the month.

(*iii*) Lowest temperature during the month and the day number on which it occured.

(*iv*) Highest temperature during the month and the day number of the month on which it occured.

4.9. To obtained the sum and the difference of two matrices.

4.10. A fishing fleet fishes in 10 different regions each consisting of 8 different areas. The data about the fish caught in kgs. are available for processing. It is required to determine

(*i*) Regionwise average fish caught.

(*ii*) Areawise average fish caught.

(*iii*) The area of the region that yielded the highest caught.

(*iv*) The area of the region that yielded the lowest caught.

(*v*) Grand total of the fish caught.

Also it is required to show the data in a tabular format.

5 THE ART OF FILE PROCESSING

INTRODUCTION

The term file may generally be defined as ***an organized collection of well-ordered, well-related and self-contained information held on a stable storage medium.***

Here the term ***'organized'*** implies that the information is placed in a specific way and read back in a definite way. The term ***'well-ordered'*** is used to mean that the information kept together as a unit must be in same sequence for the units of information in the file. The word ***'well-related'*** is used to mean that the different units of information must bear some relationship with one another for collective consideration. The term ***'self-contained'*** means that it is complete in all respect. The stable storage medium may be a piece of paper, a magnetic or optical disk or a magnetic tape or any other medium where the information can be kept for a long time for repeated use by one or different persons without any special aid. Thus the information bearing the characteristics mentioned above stored in the main memory of a computer will not make a file because the main memory of a computer can hold it as long as electricity is supplied to the main memory.

Depending on the nature of the information files can be classified into two basic types, *viz.*, the ***program file*** and the ***data file.*** The term ***program file*** implies a file that contains a sequential set of instructions in some computer language that can direct a computer in the performance of some specific task. A ***data file*** is a collection of records about closely-related and similar entities. However, these types of files should possess all the features stated in the generalised definition above. A ***record*** is an ordered collection of attribute values of an entity. An ***attribute*** is any characteristic or feature of an entity that tells something about the entity, where an entity is anything having physical or conceptual existence about which we become interested. Being interested about entities we like to collect facts about them. A ***fact*** is anything that is true about an entity. To collect facts about an entity we first decide on some attributes of the entity and procure facts on those attributes. We normally choose a group of entities called an entity set which are considered together for some close relationship. We next select some of the attributes common to all the entities of the set and collect facts on those attributes in a predefined order to form record for each of them and put all such records together to form the desired file. Let us consider a business enterprise, for instance. The employees of the enterprise forms a closely related set of entities. If we consider the attributes EMPLOYEE-CODE-NUMBER, EMPLOYEE-NAME, EMPLOYEE-ADDRESS, DESIGNATION and SALARY for each of the employees, then the values of these attributes in the mentioned order will form a record of an employee of the enterprise and the collection of all the records of the employees of the enterprise will form the desired employee data file if the records are kept on some stable storage medium.

By the term file, we normally imply a data file. So the task of file processing is the set of activities performed on the records of a file to generate some desired information. Now depending on the organization of the records, the set of operations will vary. So we next consider a discussion on the file organizations. Basically, file organizations are classified into three categories, *viz.*,

(*i*) Sequential File Organization,

(*ii*) Indexed File Organization

and (*iii*) Hashed/Relative/Random File Organization

A sequential file organization is one in which records are kept in the file one after another and processed in the same sequence in which they are written. The term sequential means one after another and hence the name bears the nature of the organization of the file.

An indexed file organization is one in which sequentially organized records are associated with an index for the purpose of direct access to the records. An index is a special kind of file that contains records consisting of two attribute values one of which is a unique identifying attribute of the records in the sequential file and the other contains the address of the records in the main file. The identifying attribute is also known as key attribute or key field. The records in the index are kept in ascending order of the key field values. When a user wishes to access a record from an indexed file, he/she initiates a binary search in the index for some key field value and the record found in the search process is then accessed to get the address of the desired record in the main file. Thus any record in an indexed file can be accessed without reading the preceding or the following records in the file. This saves time and increases the speed of processing if the number of records to be accessed in one processing run is less than one fourth of the total number of records in the file. The disadvantage of such a file organization is that it takes additional disk space for the index and hence the file organization is more expensive than the sequential file organization. The speed of accessing records also varies depending on the organization of the records in the index. For more details about the index file organization, the reader is advised to go through any standard text book on database or file management systems.

A hashed or relative file organization is also a direct access file organization. In such a file organization, the key field or identifying attribute value is hashed or converted to some location address in the file space relative to the beginning of the file-record positions on the basis of some predefined function. The predefined function is called a hash routine and the method is called hashing. As the hashing is done dynamically during the creation of the file, no extra file space is needed for this purpose, rather the records can be pointed to directly later by using the same hash function. The only problem with this type of organization is the proper selection of the hash function and its implementation through programming instructions. Programming efficiency of the developers is considered while selecting one of the two direct access file organizations. The reader is again advised to go through some text book on file/database management systems for further details. We shall now study different problems on file processing to illustrate the flowcharts and the algorithms corresponding to their solutions. The following problems are on sequential file organization.

Problem 5.1. *Construct a flowchart to show how the records of the students in a computer training institution are kept in a file. Each record consists of*

(*i*) STUDENT-ID (for unique identification of the students)
(*ii*) STUDENT-NAME
(*iii*) COURSE-NAME
(*iv*) COURSE-FEE
(*v*) FEES-PAID, and
(*vi*) DATE-OF-ADMISSION

Task Analysis. The logic of this problem is straightforward. Data will have to be accepted from the terminal for the attributes for one student at a time in the order of their specification to form a student record and then the record is to be written in the file space designated through the opening statement of a file until the user signals no more record to be written in the file. The file space is then delinked by writing a statement for closing the file. The user's signal for no more records to be written in the file can be indicated by inputting an invalid data value for the first attribute of the record, say 0 for STUDENT-ID.

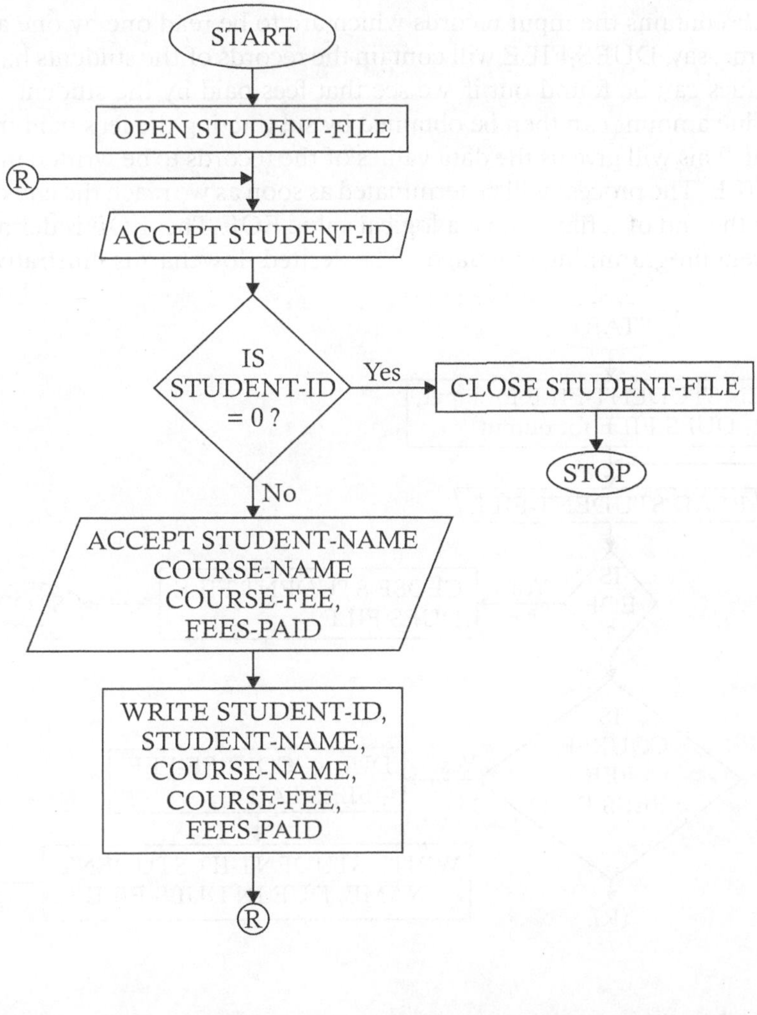

The algorithm corresponding to the above problem may be stated as under.

Step 1. OPEN STUDENT-FILE
Step 2. REPEAT STEPS 3 THROUGH 7
Step 3. ACCEPT STUDENT-ID
Step 4. IF STUDENT-ID = 0
THEN
(*i*) CLOSE STUDENT-FILE
(*ii*) EXIT
END-IF
Step 5. ACCEPT STUDENT-NAME, COURSE-NAME, COURSE-FEE, FEES-PAID
Step 6. WRITE STUDENT-RECORD
Step 7. END.

Problem 5.2. *Develop a flowchart to process the records of the STUDENT-FILE mentioned in problem 5.1 to create another file containing records of the students having dues where each record will consist of STUDENT-ID, STUDENT-NAME, and DUE-AMOUNT.*

Task Analysis. It is obvious that two files are to be used here. The first file named STUDENT-FILE contains the input records which are to be read one by one and the second file which we name, say, DUES-FILE will contain the records of the students having dues. The student having dues can be found out if we see that fees paid by the student is less than the course fee. The due amount can then be obtained by subtracting the fees paid from the course fee of the student. This will give us the data values of the records to be written in the output file named DUES-FILE. The process will be terminated as soon as we reach the end of STUDENT-FILE. We check the end of a file against a logical value EOF. The EOF is defined in a variety of ways in different programming languages. The desired flowchart is illustrated below :

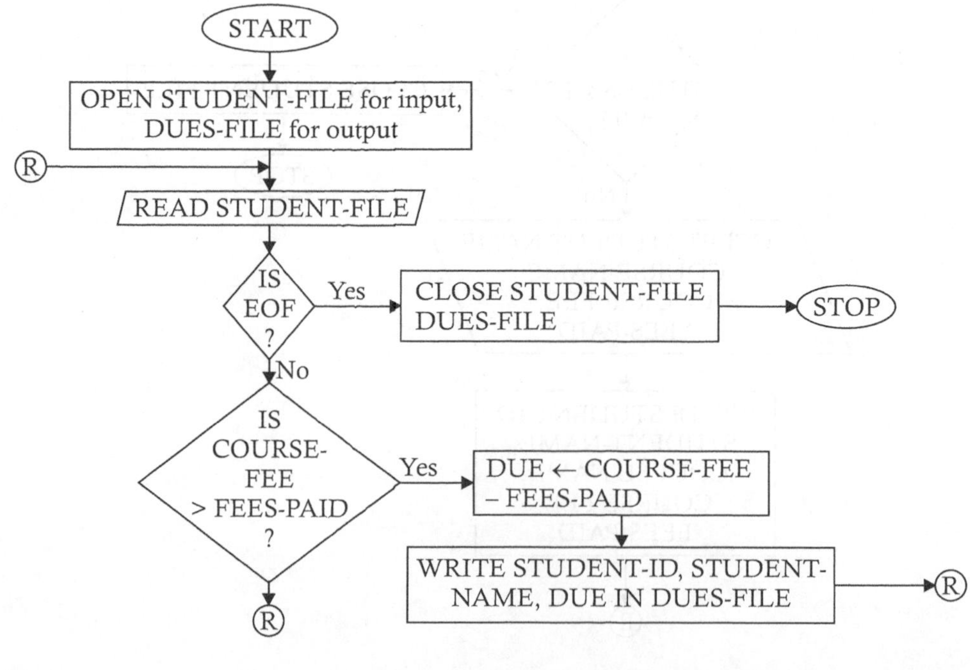

The algorithm corresponding to the above problem is stated below :

Step 1. OPEN INPUT STUDENT-FILE, OUTPUT DUES-FILE

Step 2. REPEAT STEPS 3 THROUGH 5

Step 3. READ A RECORD FROM STUDENT-FILE

Step 4. IF EOF OF STUDENT-FILE
THEN
(*i*) CLOSE STUDENT-FILE
(*ii*) EXIT
END-IF

Step 5. IF COURSE-FEE > FEES-PAID
THEN DUE ← COURSE-FEE – FEES-PAID
WRITE STUDENT-ID, STUDENT-NAME, DUE IN DUES-FILE
END-IF

Step 6. STOP

Step 7. END.

Problem 5.3. *A file named EMPFL contains records of employees of an organization. Each record consists of data on EMP-CODE, EMP-NAME, and BASIC-PAY. The gross salary of an employee is calculated by using the following formula : Gross Salary = Basic-pay + DA + ADA + HRA + MA*

where DA = 45% of Basic Pay

ADA = 18% of Basic Pay subject to a minimum of Rs. 200 and a maximum of Rs. 1000.

HRA = 25% of Basic Pay subject to a minimum of Rs. 500 and a maximum of Rs. 5000.

MA = 10% of Basic pay subject to a minimum of Rs. 100.

The net salary of an employee is calculated by the formula :

Net Salary = Gross Salary – Total Deduction

where Total Deduction = PF + PT

where PF = 12% of Basic Pay

PT = 5% of Basic Pay subject to a maximum of Rs. 200.

Develop a flowchart and then the algorithm to show how salary for different employees is calculated to generate pay-slips for the employees of the organization.

Task Analysis. The problem here is to print payslip for each of the employees whose records are contained in the EMPFL. This can be done by reading the records of the employees one at a time and then calculating the DA, ADA, HRA and MA values to determine the gross salary and then finding out the amounts of PF and PT for determining the total deduction. The net salary can then be obtained by subtracting the total deduction from the gross salary. Now the calculation of ADA needs additional observation. It is stated that the ADA, will be 18% of Basic Pay subject to a minimum of Rs. 200 and a maximum of Rs. 1000. This implies that if the 18% of Basic Pay value happens to be less than Rs. 200, then Rs. 200 is to be taken as the ADA amount; if, however, it exceeds Rs. 1000, then Rs. 1000 is to be taken as the ADA amount. Similarly the conditions for HRA, MA and PT can be handled. The following flowchart depicts the procedure step by step :

```
Step 8.  COMPUTE HRA ← BASIC-PAY * .25
Step 9.  IF HRA < 500
            THEN HRA ← 5000
         ELSE
         IF HRA > 5000
            THEN HRA ← 5000
         END-IF
         END-IF
Step 10. COMPUTE MA ← BASIC-PAY * .10
Step 11. IF MA < 100
            THEN MA ← 100
         END-IF
Step 12. COMPUTE PF ← BASIC-PAY * .12
Step 13. COMPUTE PT ← BASIC PAY * .05
Step 14. IF PT > 200
            THEN PT  ← 200
         END-IF
Step 15. COMPUTE GROSS-PAY ← BASIC-PAY + DA + ADA + HRA + MA
Step 16. COMPUTE TD ← PF + PT
Step 17. COMPUTE NET-PAY ← GROSS-PAY – TD
Step 18. PRINT EMPCODE,
         EMPNAME,
         GROSS-PAY, TD,
         NET-PAY
Step 19. STOP
```

Problem 5.4. *A file named INVENT contains records of assets in the inventory of a company for the computation and printing of depreciation schedule for each of them. Each record consists of ASSET-MEMBER, ASSET-VALUE, RATE, YEARS, where RATE contains the rate of depreciation and YEARS contains the life-span of the asset over which the asset will be depreciated. The following table illustrates the desired form of the output for some asset.*

ASSET	*45678*	*ORIGINAL VALUE RS. 1000.00*	*RATE 0.20*
YEAR	*DEPRECIATION*	*ACCUMULATED DEPRECIATION*	*BOOK VALUE*
1	*Rs. 200.00*	*Rs. 200.00*	*Rs. 800.00*
2	*160.00*	*360.00*	*640.00*
3	*128.00`*	*488.00*	*512.00*
4	*102.40*	*590.00*	*409.00*
5	*89.92*	*672.32*	*327.68*

Construct a flowchart to show the processing logic of the problem. Also develop the algorithm of the solution.

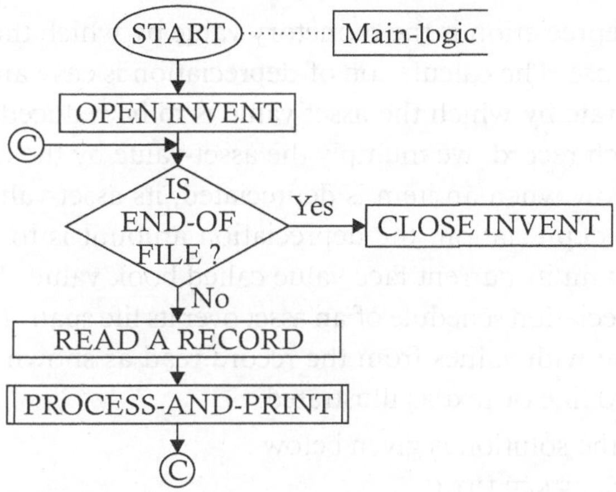
START
Main-logic
OPEN INVENT
C
IS
END-OF
FILE ?
Yes
CLOSE INVENT
No
READ A RECORD
PROCESS-AND-PRINT
C

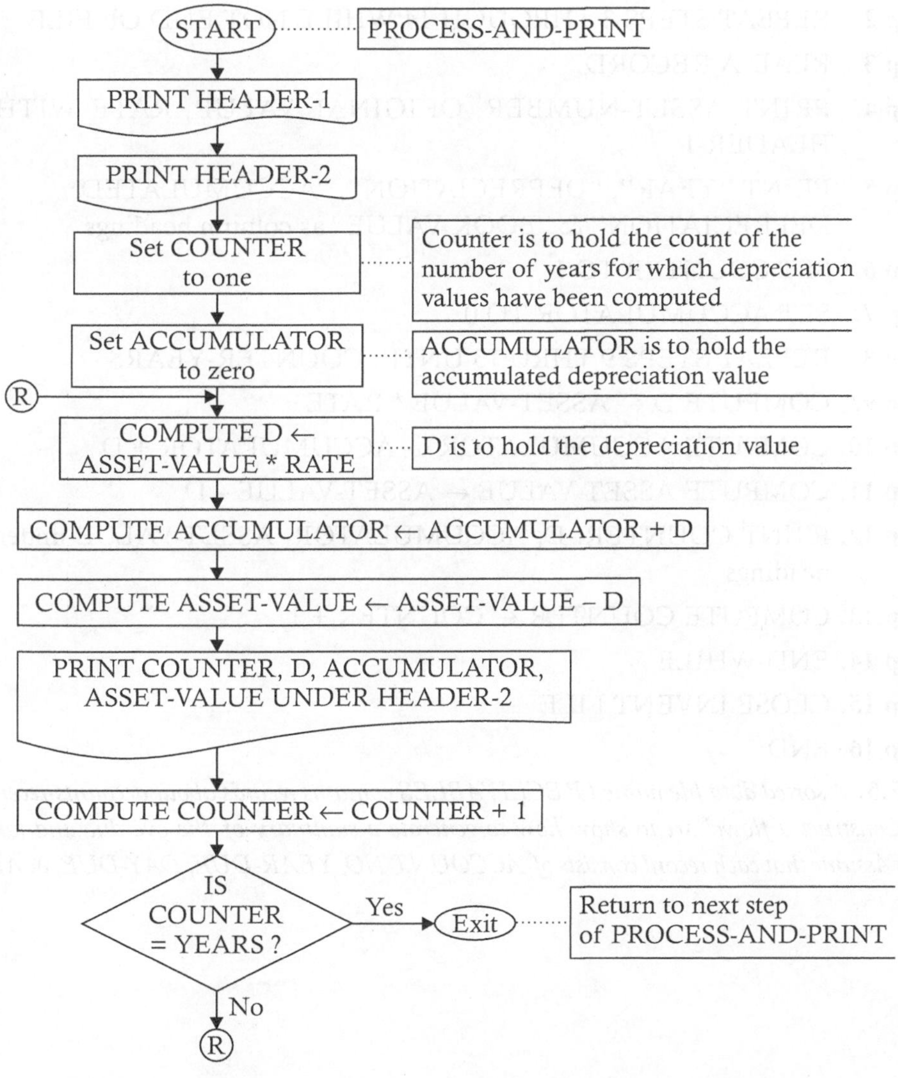
START
PROCESS-AND-PRINT
PRINT HEADER-1
PRINT HEADER-2
Set COUNTER to one
Counter is to hold the count of the number of years for which depreciation values have been computed
Set ACCUMULATOR to zero
ACCUMULATOR is to hold the accumulated depreciation value
R
COMPUTE D ← ASSET-VALUE * RATE
D is to hold the depreciation value
COMPUTE ACCUMULATOR ← ACCUMULATOR + D
COMPUTE ASSET-VALUE ← ASSET-VALUE – D
PRINT COUNTER, D, ACCUMULATOR, ASSET-VALUE UNDER HEADER-2
COMPUTE COUNTER ← COUNTER + 1
IS
COUNTER
= YEARS ?
Yes
Exit
Return to next step of PROCESS-AND-PRINT
No
R

Task Analysis. Depreciation is the monetory value by which the value of some asset is reduced for each year of use. The calculation of depreciation is easy and straightforward here. The asset-value and the rate by which the asset-value is to be reduced are both given in each record. So by reading each record, we multiply the asset-value by the rate to obtain its current value of depreciation. Now when an item is depreciated, its asset-value gets decreased, so to compute the next year's depreciation, the depreciation amount is to be subtracted from the current asset-value to obtain its current face value called book value. This calculation is to be repeated to print the depreciation schedule of an asset over its life span. The HEADER-1 implies the first line of text along with values from the record read as shown in the illustration. The HEADER-2 is the second line of text as illustrated.

The algorithm of the solution is given below :

Step 1. OPEN INVENT FILE

Step 2. REPEAT STEPS 3 THROUGH 14 WHILE NOT END OF FILE

Step 3. READ A RECORD

Step 4. PRINT ASSET-NUMBER, ORIGINAL-VALUE, RATE WITH text as HEADER-1

Step 5. PRINT "YEAR", "DEPRECIATION", "ACCUMULATED DEPRECIATION" & "BOOK VALUE" as column headings

Step 6. SET COUNTER TO 1

Step 7. SET ACCUMULATOR TO 0

Step 8. REPEAT STEPS 9 THRU 13 UNTIL COUNTER-YEARS

Step 9. COMPUTE D ← ASSET-VALUE * RATE

Step 10. COMPUTE ACCUMULATOR ← ACCUMULATOR + D

Step 11. COMPUTE ASSET-VALUE ← ASSET-VALUE – D

Step 12. PRINT COUNTER, D, ACCUMULATOR, ASSET-VALUE under column headings

Step 13. COMPUTE COUNTER ← COUNTER + 1

Step 14. END-WHILE

Step 15. CLOSE INVENT FILE

Step 16. END.

Problem 5.5. *A sorted data file named RECEIVABLES contains records about accounts-receivable of a company. Construct a flowchart to show how to generate a summary of the overdue and forthcoming receivables. Assume that each record consists of ACCOUNT-NO, YEAR-DUE, DAY-DUE, & AMOUNT-DUE.*

Task Analysis. Obviously, the datafile is to be kept sorted in ascending sequence of ACCOUNT-NO. We may assume that there is only one record per account. To print the desired output the current (today's) date and year should be accepted from the terminal or from the system as the user likes. We suggest to print the account number in the output which is found to be out of sequence as shown in the sample output below :

ACCOUNT OUT OF SEQUENCE 005367		
STATUS	*NUMBER OF ACCOUNTS*	*VALUE (IN RS.)*
OVERDUE	05	10,000.00
RECEIVABLE	03	5,000.00
TOTALS	02	15,000.00

The flowchart of the program logic is shown below :

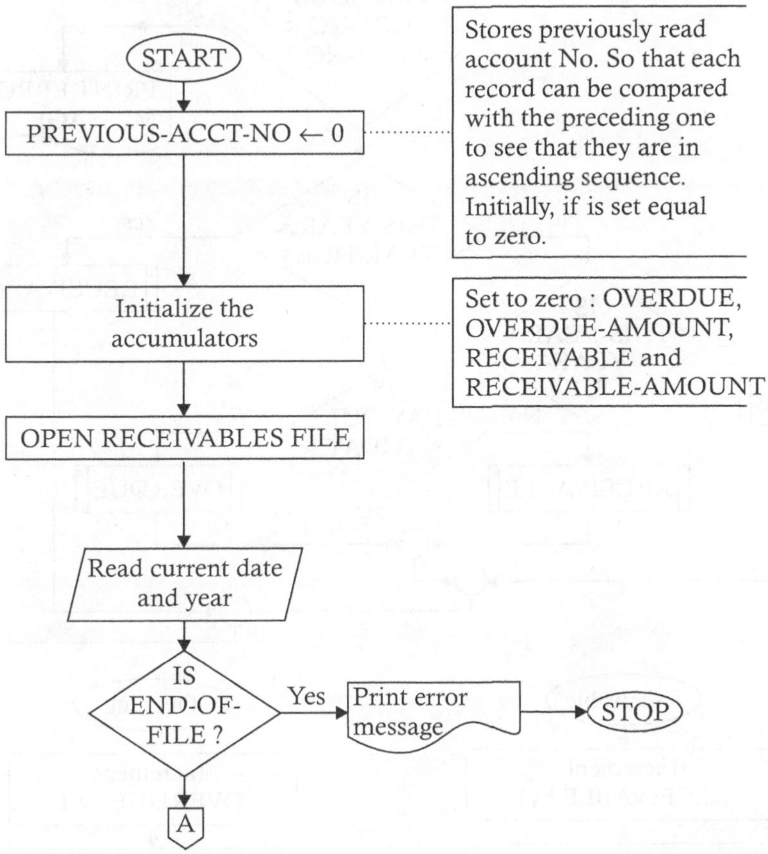

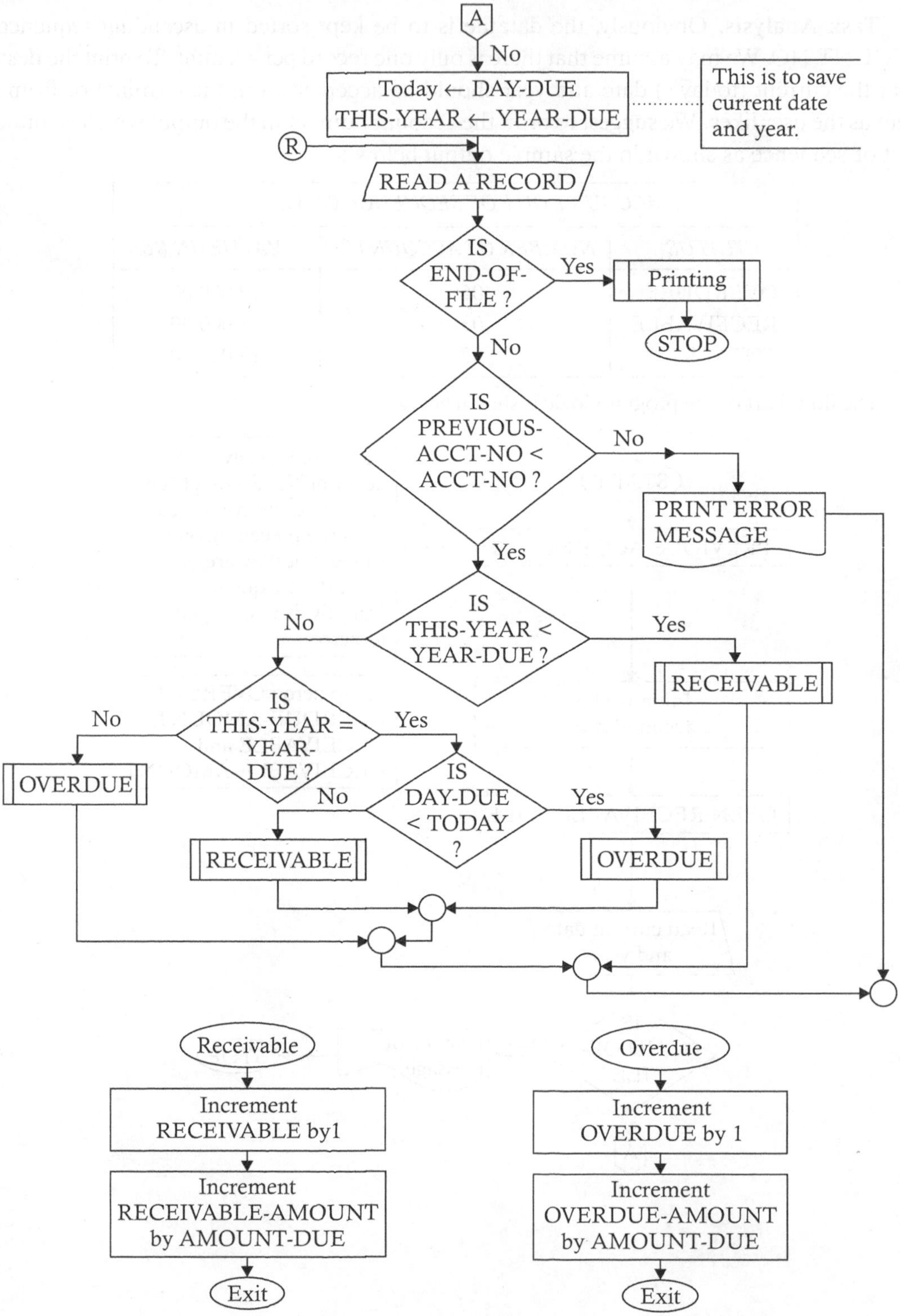
A
No
Today ← DAY-DUE
THIS-YEAR ← YEAR-DUE
This is to save current date and year.
R
READ A RECORD
IS END-OF-FILE ?
Yes
Printing
STOP
No
IS PREVIOUS-ACCT-NO < ACCT-NO ?
No
PRINT ERROR MESSAGE
Yes
IS THIS-YEAR < YEAR-DUE ?
No
Yes
RECEIVABLE
IS THIS-YEAR = YEAR-DUE ?
No
Yes
OVERDUE
IS DAY-DUE < TODAY ?
No
Yes
RECEIVABLE
OVERDUE
Receivable
Increment RECEIVABLE by1
Increment RECEIVABLE-AMOUNT by AMOUNT-DUE
Exit
Overdue
Increment OVERDUE by 1
Increment OVERDUE-AMOUNT by AMOUNT-DUE
Exit

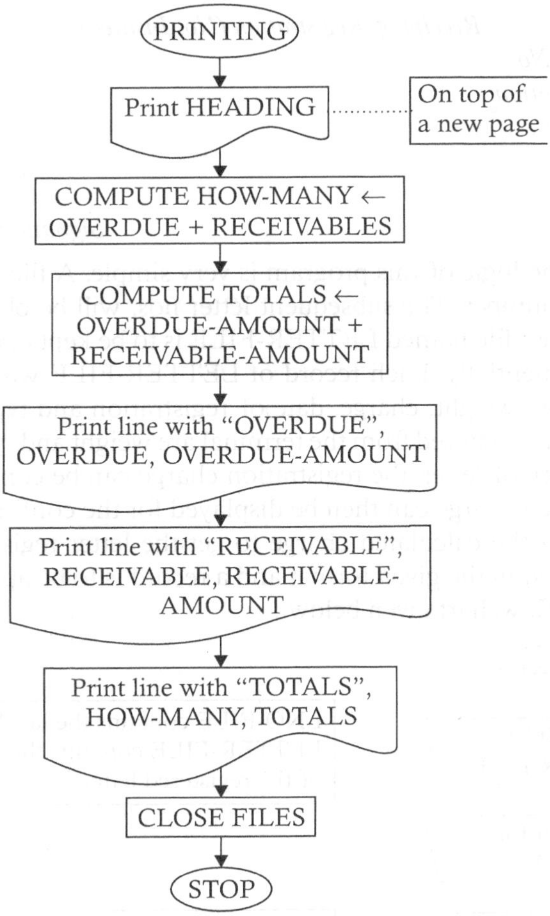

Problem 5.6. *The registration charge on letters is calculated as per the following rules :*

For the first 20 gms or part thereof the charge is fixed and it is equal to Rs. 8.25 for inland letters and Rs. 25.75 for foreign letters.

For the next every additional 15 gms or part thereof the charge is Rs. 7.25 for inland letters and Rs. 18.25 for foreign letters until the gross weight does not exceed 500 gms.

For weights beyond 500 gms, the charge is calculated at the rate Rs. 1.65 per gm for inland letters and at the rate of Rs. 4.65 per foreign letters.

Develop a flowchart for the following :

(i) To accept weight and type of letter interactively to calculate the charge and then to display it ;

and *(ii) If the sender agrees to register at the calculated charge, add a record to a register file consisting of letter no., destination, weight, charge, date of registration and letter type and then print out a receipt for the sender in the following format :*

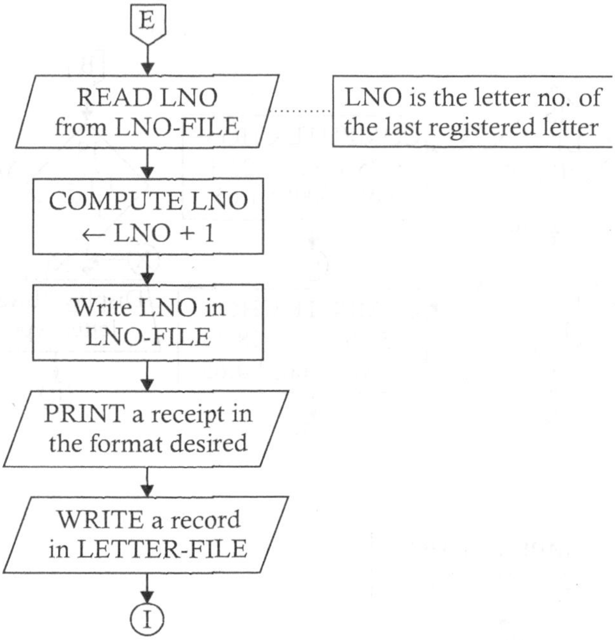

In the above flowchart, the computation of 15 gms intervals has been done by using the following formula :

$$\text{INV} = \text{integer part of } \frac{(\text{Excess Weight} - 1)}{15} + 1$$

The reader can check the validity of the formula for any additional weight. The algorithm of the above procedure is stated below :

Step 1. OPEN LNO-FILE, LETTER-FILE

Step 2. REPEAT STEP 3 THROUGH 15

Step 3. ACCEPT W from the terminal [W is the weight of a letter desired to be registered]

Step 4. IF W <= 0 THEN EXIT

Step 5. ACCEPT LT from the terminal [LT is the type of letter-Inland or Foreign]

Step 6. IF W <= 20

THEN IF LT = "I"

THEN CHG ← 8.25

ELSE IF LT = "F"

THEN CHG ← 25.75

ELSE

PRINT "INVALID LETTER TYPE"

GO TO STEP 5

END-IF

END-IF

```
ELSE IF W <= 500
        THEN COMPUTE EW ← W – 500
        COMPUTE INV ← INT((EW – 1)/15) + 1
IF LT = "I"
        THEN COMPUTE CHG ← 8.25 + INV * 7.25
ELSE IF LT = "F"
        THEN COMPUTE CHG ← 25.75 + INV * 18.25
        ELSE PRINT "INVALID LETTER TYPE"
          GO TO STEP 5
        END-IF
        END-IF
ELSE IF LT = "I"
        THEN COMPUTE CHG ← 8.25 + 32 * 7.25 + (W – 500) * 1.65
ELSE IF LT = "F"
        THEN COMPUTE CHG ← 18.75 + 32 * 18.25 + (W – 500) * 4.65
        ELSE PRINT "INVALID LETTER TYPE " GO TO SETP 5
END-IF
END-IF
END-IF
Step 7.  DISPLAY CHG
Step 8.  ACCEPT RESPONSE
         (TO DETERMINE WHETHER THE SENDER WISHES TO REGISTER
         AT THE CALCULATED CHARGE or NOT)
Step 9.  IF RESPONSE = "N"
         THEN GO TO STEP 3
         END-IF
Step 10. ACCEPT DESTINATION from the terminal
Step 11. READ LNO from LNO-FILE
Step 12. COMPUTE LNO ← LNO + 1
         (Generate new LNO)
Step 13. PRINT RECEIPT
Step 14. WRITE a record in LETTER-FILE
Step 15. END-REPEAT
Step 16. END
```

Problem 5.7. *ABC university conducted an examination and collected the students' personal data and the total marks obtained in the examination in a file named STUDENTS. The record layout is given below :*

Data Description	*Data Type & Size*
Roll Number	*5 numeric*
Name of the Student	*25 alphabetic*
Sex Code (M : Male F : Female)	*1 alphabetic*
Marital Status Code (U : Unmarried ; M : Married, D : Divorced ; W : Widowed)	*1 alphabetic*
Age in Years	*2 numeric*
Total Marks Obtained	*3 numeric*

The university authorities required the students' result in printed form having the following information for each student :

1. Roll Number
2. Title of the Student (MR/MISS/MRS.)
3. Name of the Student
4. Age in Years
5. Total Marks Obtained
6. Result (PASSED/FAILED)
7. Grade (EXCELLENT/VERY GOOD/ GOOD/ FAIR/POOR)

At the end of the results of all the students, the following summary is to be provided :

SUMMARISED INFORMATION

SEX	*PASSED*					*FAILED*	*TOTAL NO. OF*
	EXCELLENT	*V. GOOD*	*GOOD*	*FAIR*	*TOTAL*	*POOR*	*STUDENTS APPEARED*
NO. OF GIRLS							
NO. OF BOYS							

The following criteria were adopted for declaring the result and grade of the students :

Marks Obtained	*Result*	*Grade*
≥ 900	Passed	Excellent
<900 but ≥ 750	Passed	Very Good
< 750 but ≥ 500	Passed	Good
< 500 but ≤ 400	Passed	Fair
< 400	Failed	Poor

The criteria for generating the title of each student is taken as follows :

1. If the sex code is 'M' then the title is "MR"
2. If the sex code is 'F' and the marital status is 'U' then the title is "MISS"
3. If the sex code is 'F' and the marital status is "M" or "D" or "W" then the title is "MRS.".

Construct a flowchart to show the processing logic of the STUDENTS file to get the information desired.

Show the algorithm of the solution.

Task Analysis. The problem consists of two major activities, namely, (*i*) developing the result, grade, and the title of each student for the given data, and printing the information in the desired format ; and (*ii*) obtaining the summary totals to be printed at the end of the processing to all students data.

The title of a student is generated from the combination of sex code and the marital status code as per the criteria stated in the problem statement. The result and the grade of the student is developed from the marks obtained as per the criteria stated. Depending upon the sex code and the grade, the summary controls are developed. Lastly, the required information is printed. The steps-involved in the entire processing task have been shown pictorially in the flowchart below :

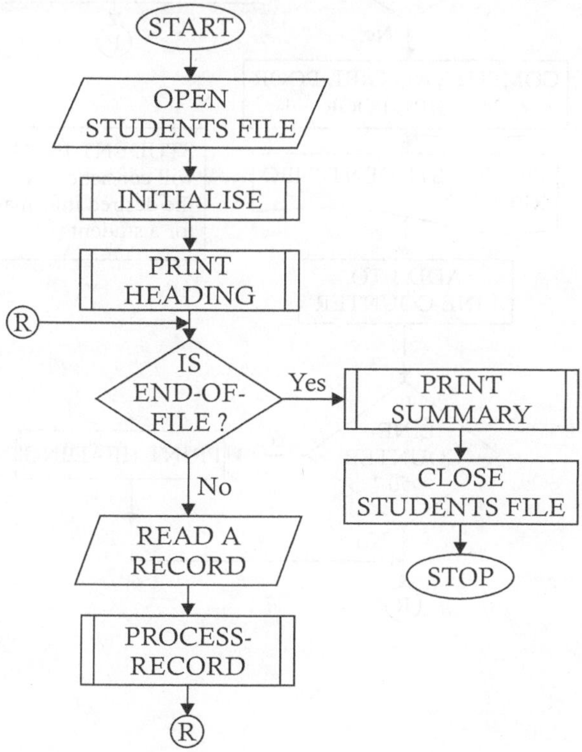

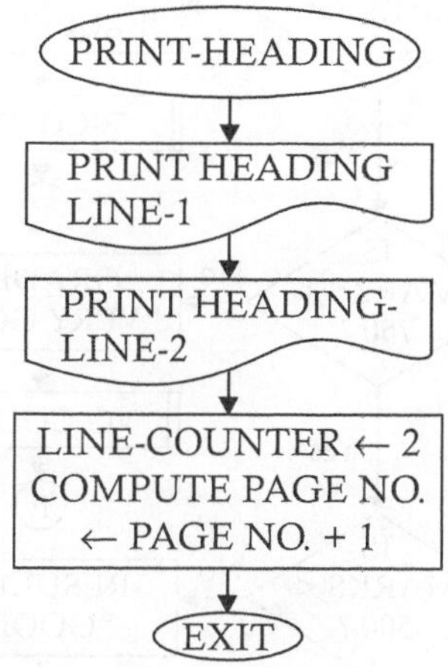

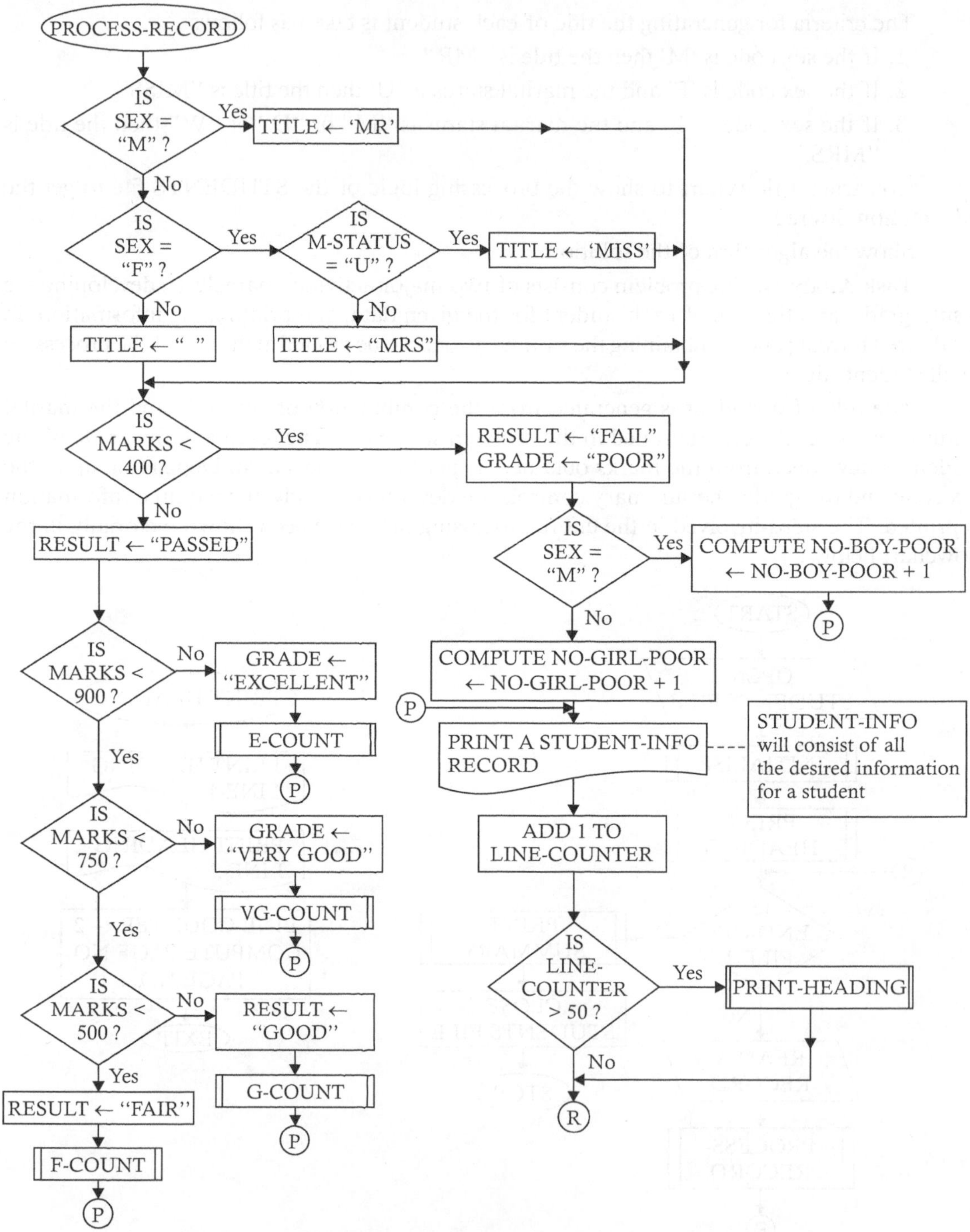
PROCESS-RECORD
IS SEX = "M" ?
Yes
TITLE ← 'MR'
No
IS SEX = "F" ?
Yes
IS M-STATUS = "U" ?
Yes
TITLE ← 'MISS'
No
No
TITLE ← " "
TITLE ← "MRS"
IS MARKS < 400 ?
Yes
RESULT ← "FAIL"
GRADE ← "POOR"
No
RESULT ← "PASSED"
IS SEX = "M" ?
Yes
COMPUTE NO-BOY-POOR ← NO-BOY-POOR + 1
P
No
COMPUTE NO-GIRL-POOR ← NO-GIRL-POOR + 1
P
IS MARKS < 900 ?
No
GRADE ← "EXCELLENT"
E-COUNT
P
Yes
PRINT A STUDENT-INFO RECORD
STUDENT-INFO will consist of all the desired information for a student
IS MARKS < 750 ?
No
GRADE ← "VERY GOOD"
VG-COUNT
P
Yes
ADD 1 TO LINE-COUNTER
IS LINE-COUNTER > 50 ?
Yes
PRINT-HEADING
No
R
IS MARKS < 500 ?
No
RESULT ← "GOOD"
G-COUNT
P
Yes
RESULT ← "FAIR"
F-COUNT
P

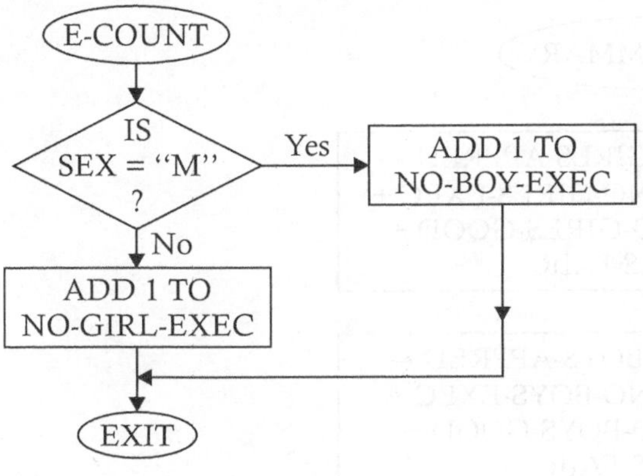
E-COUNT
IS
SEX = "M"
?
Yes
ADD 1 TO
NO-BOY-EXEC
No
ADD 1 TO
NO-GIRL-EXEC
EXIT

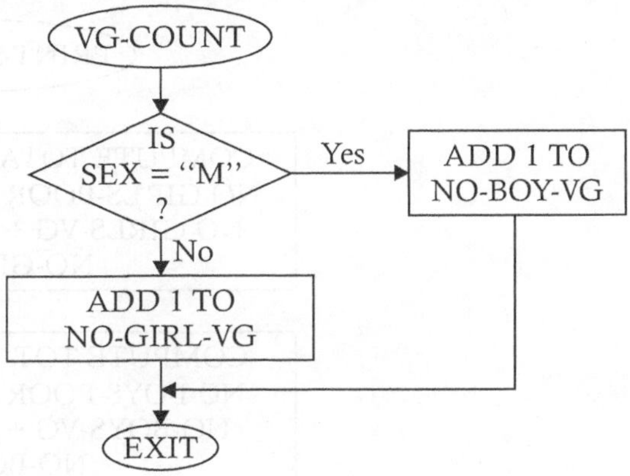
VG-COUNT
IS
SEX = "M"
?
Yes
ADD 1 TO
NO-BOY-VG
No
ADD 1 TO
NO-GIRL-VG
EXIT

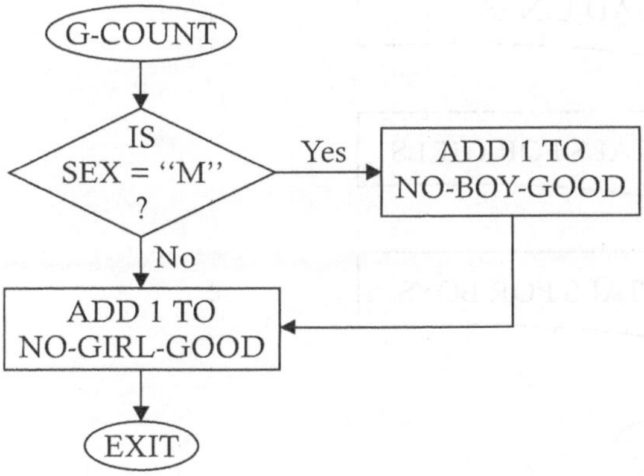
G-COUNT
IS
SEX = "M"
?
Yes
ADD 1 TO
NO-BOY-GOOD
No
ADD 1 TO
NO-GIRL-GOOD
EXIT

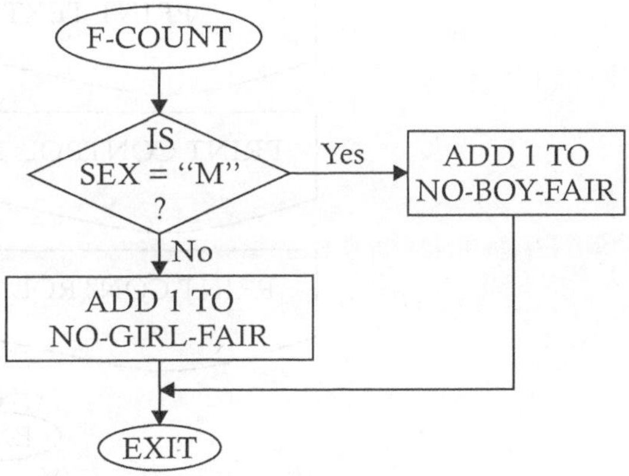
F-COUNT
IS
SEX = "M"
?
Yes
ADD 1 TO
NO-BOY-FAIR
No
ADD 1 TO
NO-GIRL-FAIR
EXIT

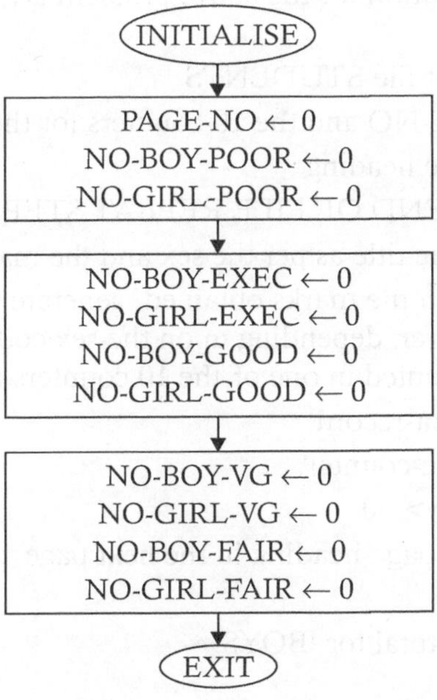
INITIALISE
PAGE-NO ← 0
NO-BOY-POOR ← 0
NO-GIRL-POOR ← 0
NO-BOY-EXEC ← 0
NO-GIRL-EXEC ← 0
NO-BOY-GOOD ← 0
NO-GIRL-GOOD ← 0
NO-BOY-VG ← 0
NO-GIRL-VG ← 0
NO-BOY-FAIR ← 0
NO-GIRL-FAIR ← 0
EXIT

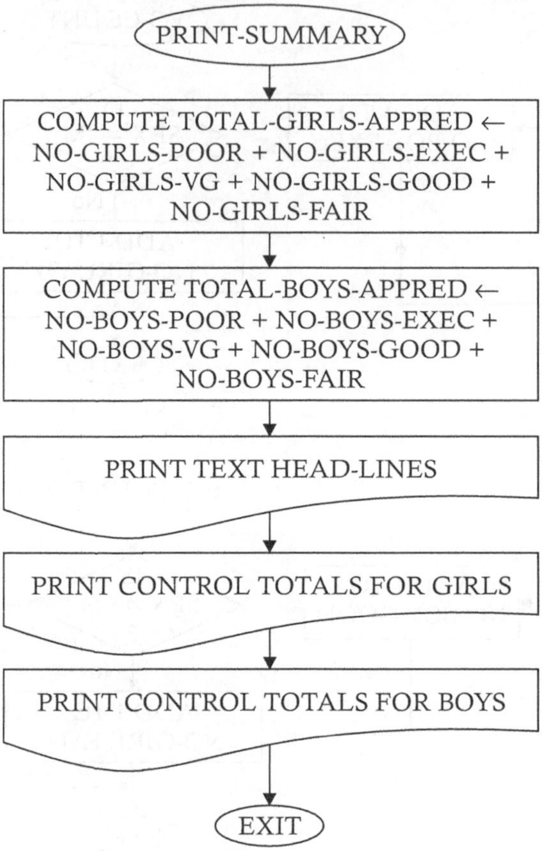

The algorithm of the solution for the above problem is given in the following steps in a summarised form :

Step 1. OPEN the input file STUDENTS

Step 2. Initialize PAGE-NO and the 10 counters for the summary information

Step 3. PRINT the page heading

Step 4. WHILE NOT END OF FILE REPEAT STEP 5 THROUGH STEP 9

Step 5. GENERATE the title as per the sex and the marital status code

Step 6. Depending upon the marks obtained, generate the grade and the result of the student. Moreover, depending upon the sex code and the grade of the student the record is counted in one of the 10 counters for the summary.

Step 7. PRINT a student-record

Step 8. ADD 1 TO Line-counter

Step 9. IF Line-counter > 50
THEN PRINT page-heading in the next page
END-IF

Step 10. CALCULATE total for 'BOYS'

Step 11. CALCULATE total for 'GIRLS'
Step 12. PRINT total for 'BOYS'
Step 13. PRINT total for 'GIRLS'
Step 14. CLOSE STUDENT file
Step 15. STOP

Problem 5.8. *A branch of a nationalised bank (called ABC Bank) has computerised the savings bank account of its consumers. As a result they are giving a monthly statement to the customers stating their transactions during every month.*

The data relating to the names and address of the customer, Savings Bank Account No. and opening balance for every month are kept in a disk file called SBMAST.DAT. This file is sorted in the order of S.B. Account Number. All the transaction for the customers are entered in another file called SBTRAN.DAT. At the end of every month, the transaction file is sorted on S.B. Account Number and matched with the Master file for the printing out detailed statement for each customer.

The format of the two input files are given below :

SBMAST-DAT

Data Name	Description	Type & Size
BR-CODE	Branch Code	4 AN
SB-ACT-NO	Account Number	10 AN
NAME	Name of Customer	25 AN
ADDR	Address	30 AN
OPENING BALANCE	Opening balance at the beginning of month	N(7 + 2)

Savings Bank Transaction File : SBTRAN.DAT

Data Name	Description	Type & Size
SB-ACT-NO	Account Number	10 AN
TR-DAT	Transaction Date	8 AN
DESCRN	Description	15 AN
DEBIT	Withdrawals	(6 + 2) N
CREDIT	Deposits	(6 + 2) N

The name and address of the customer would be printed as taken from the Master file. The S/B A/c Number would be printed on the top right hand side.

The closing balance of the account would be the opening balance credit-debit.

Please note the following for writing a correct programme :

There would be one record in the S.B. Master file for each customer. In the transaction file, there may be no records (for a customer who has not had any transactions during the month) or there may be multiple records, if a customer has more than one transaction during the month. In the case of accounts with no transactions the opening balance and closing balance and closing balance (both would be the same) would be printed on consecutive lines. The remarks column would contain the message "NO TRANSACTIONS", in the closing balance line. For all customers who have had transactions, every transaction would be printed as a separate line, the opening balance being the first line. The opening balance line would contain the words "OPENING BALANCE" in the description column of the line. The last line would contain the final closing balance, with the words "OPENING BALANCE" in the description column of the line. The last line would contain the final closing balance, with the words "Closing Balance" in the description column. No dates would be printed in the opening balance lines.

The data printed on the report for each transaction would be in the DD-MM-YY format. The transactions are to be printed double-spaced with 30 lines per page. There should be a page-skip after every customer transactions are printed. The page number should be initialized after every customer transactions are printed.

The month and year of statement would be taken from the terminal at a beginning of the programme.

Normally, there should be no instance of the closing balance becoming negative for any customer. If however, the closing balance becomes negative, the balance should be printed with a negative sign and an error message "BALANCE NEGATIVE" should be printed in the remarks column.

In the case of a customer, who has only transactions, but no corresponding record in the Master file, the records should be bypassed, with a message on the terminal, "NO MASTER FOR S/B ACCOUNT NO" : and the S/B Account Number should be displayed by the side.

Use only the standard file-names for the input, and output and the data-names as specific above, in the input files. In the case of print record and other intermediate values that may be required, use the following standard names :

Print Record :	SBPRT-REC	
Data Names :	RPT-DATE	Data of Transaction
	RPT-EES	Description of Transaction
	RPT-OB	Opening Balance
	RPT-CR	Credit
	RPT-DR	Debit
	RPT-CB	Closing Balance
	REMK	Remarks

Other Data Names : CUMBAL Cumulative balance starting from opening balance to which credits would be added and debit subtracted for arriving at closing balance.

MSG1	"OPENING BALANCE"
MSG2	"CLOSING BALANCE"
MSG3	"NO TRANSACTIONS"
MSG4	"BALANCE NEGATIVE"
MSG5	"NO MASTER FOR S/B ACCOUNT NO" :
PG	Page Number
MY	Month & Year accepted from terminal.

In case it becomes necessary to use any other data name other than what have been given above, a comment statement explaining what the data name stands for should be given.

Draw a rough flowchart showing the processing logic. Write comment statements to explain processing logic wherever required within the programme.

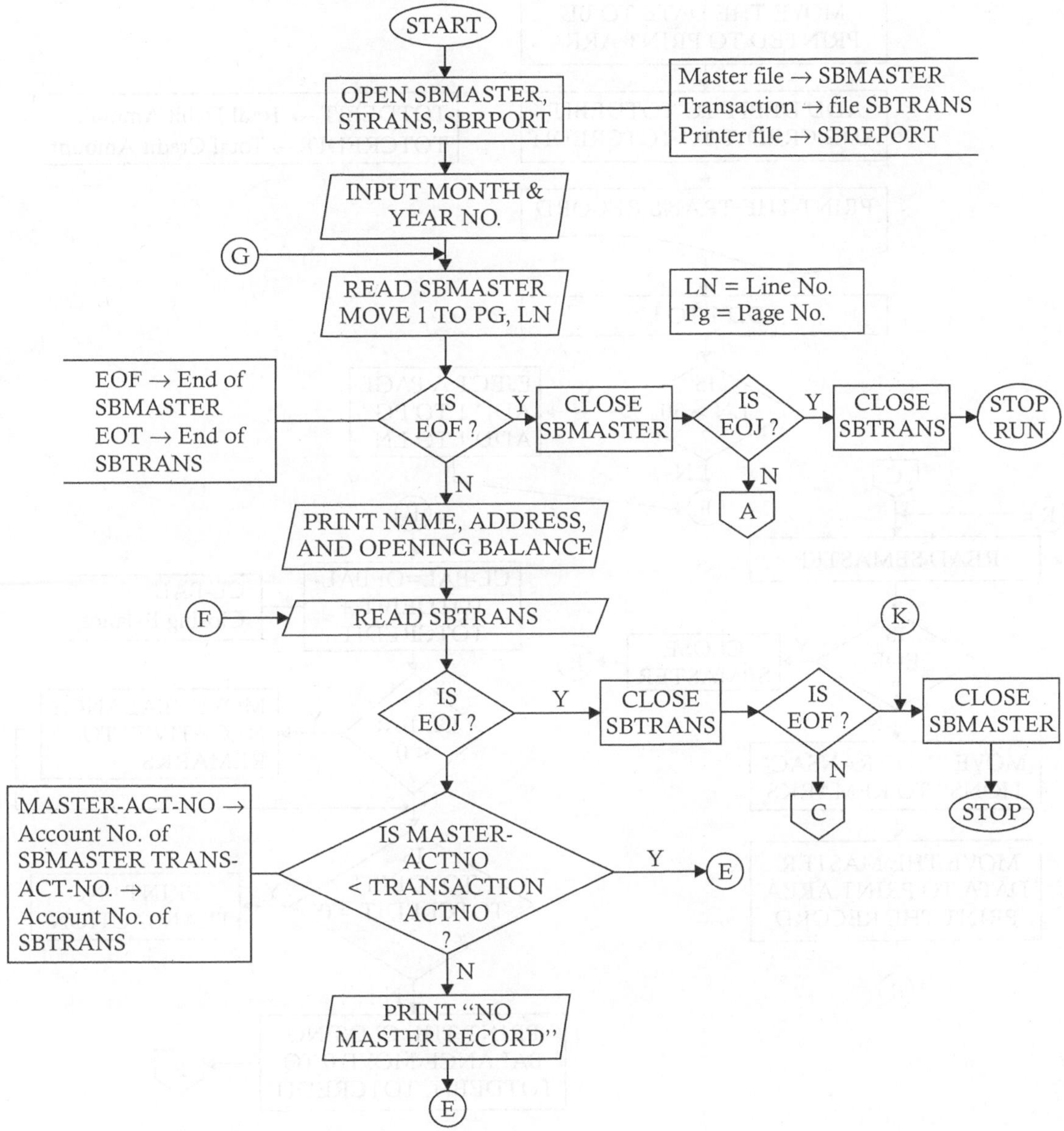

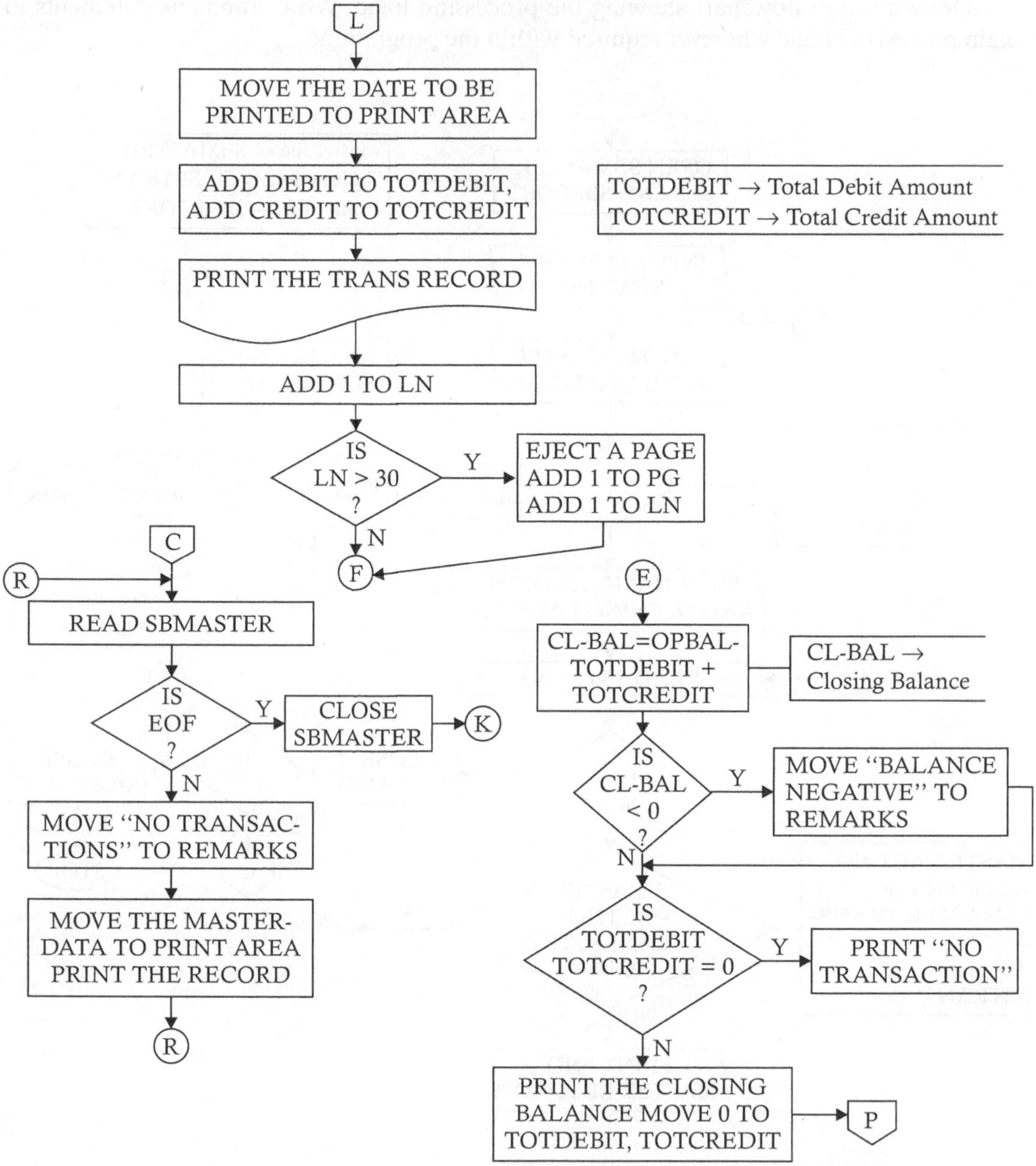
L
MOVE THE DATE TO BE PRINTED TO PRINT AREA
ADD DEBIT TO TOTDEBIT, ADD CREDIT TO TOTCREDIT
TOTDEBIT → Total Debit Amount
TOTCREDIT → Total Credit Amount
PRINT THE TRANS RECORD
ADD 1 TO LN
IS LN > 30 ?
Y
EJECT A PAGE ADD 1 TO PG ADD 1 TO LN
N
F
C
R
READ SBMASTER
IS EOF ?
Y
CLOSE SBMASTER
K
N
MOVE "NO TRANSACTIONS" TO REMARKS
MOVE THE MASTER-DATA TO PRINT AREA PRINT THE RECORD
R
E
CL-BAL=OPBAL-TOTDEBIT + TOTCREDIT
CL-BAL → Closing Balance
IS CL-BAL < 0 ?
Y
MOVE "BALANCE NEGATIVE" TO REMARKS
N
IS TOTDEBIT TOTCREDIT = 0 ?
Y
PRINT "NO TRANSACTION"
N
PRINT THE CLOSING BALANCE MOVE 0 TO TOTDEBIT, TOTCREDIT
P

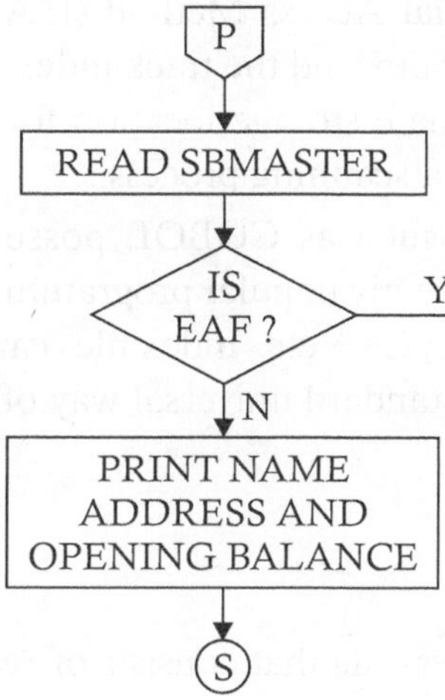

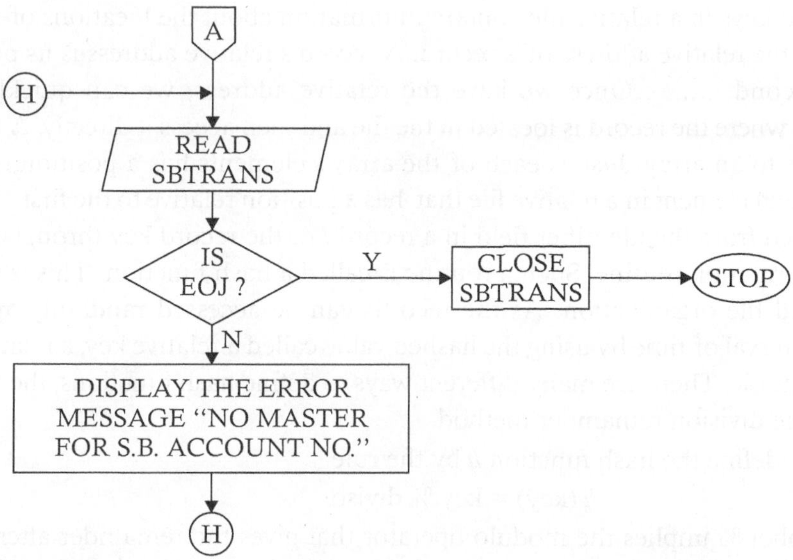

INDEXED FILE ORGANIZATION

An indexed file is a direct access file and hence it is to be created only on a disk. This file organization allows sequential storage of records but facilitates random accessing or processing. An indexed file consists of two principal components : The main file and the index. The main file contains records in sequential order. The index or index file contains records basically consisting of two fields : The first field is the key field and the second field is the address field that holds the address of the physical location of the record in the main file. The records in the index are kept in ascending sequence of key field values of the records. A particular type of an indexed file is IBM's Indexed Sequential Access Method (ISAM) file. It uses an index file consisting of two levels : The cylinder index and the track index. A search method utilizes the index tables to determine the approximate storage location for a given record and then the desired record can be accessed through a scanning process.

Some programming languages such as COBOL possess features for creation and maintenance of an indexed file. The currently popular programming languages such as C, C++ do not possess any such features. So in C, C++ etc. index files can be organized through actual coding for the purpose . As there is no standard universal way of doing this, I am not going to illustrate the use of indexed files.

RELATIVE FILE ORGANIZATION

A relative file is also a direct access file that consists of records identified by a key that contains information about the location of a record in the file. In an indexed file the identifier key has to be looked up in the table in order to determine the location of a record in the file. In contrast, record keys in a relative file contain information about the locations of records. This information is the relative address of a record. A record's relative address is its position in the file : First, second, ... Once we have the relative address, we can quickly determine approximately where the record is located in the file and then access it directly. A relative file is thus analogous to an array. Just as each of the array's elements has a position relative to the first, so is for each element in a relative file that has a position relative to the first. A relative key value is obtained from the identifier field in a record *i.e.,* the record key through some key-to-address transformation routine. Such a routine is called a hash function. This is why it is also called a hashed file organization. As the records can be accessed randomly approximately within same interval of time by using the hashed value called a relative key, a relative file is also called a random file. There are many different ways to define hash functions, the most popular one is called the division remainder method.

Here we define the hash function h by the rule

$$h\,(\text{key}) = \text{key} \ \% \ \text{divisor}$$

where the symbol % implies the modulo operator that gives the remainder after dividing the record key by divisor. The divisor selected is the largest prime number less than the maximum file size defined. Normally the file size is increased by 25% from that is actually required. Problems arise when two distinct record keys hash to the same relative storage address. Such a phenomenon is called a **collision** and the address for which the collision occurs is called a **synonym.** The file size is increased by 25% to reduce the chance of collisions. Any hashing system must provide a collision resolution policy—a way of handling collisions. We choose a collision resolution policy known as linear probing. When a collision occurs, we scan the following record locations until we find the first vacant location and store the record there (with the first record position assumed to follow the last record position). When retrieving a record, we retrieve the record in the original location ; if it is not the one we want, we keep searching in succeeding locations until we get the record identified by its key.

EXERCISE 5

5.1. Draw a flowchart to show how SALESFILE is created by accepting data from the terminal for each record. The record will consist of code number of a Salesperson, Name of the person, and Sales amount of a month.

State the algorithm of the solution.

5.2. Consider the SALESFILE created in problem 1. Construct a flowchart showing how a sales report is generated in the format outlined below :

SALES REPORT OF XYZ LTD.
FOR THE MONTH OF DECEMBER 2004

SALES PERSON CODE	*NAME*	*SALES-AMOUNT*	*COMMISSION*
IOL001	SWAPAN SEN	10,000	3,500
		⋮	⋮
	GRAND TOTALS :	...	...
NET SALES :		...	...
AVERAGE NET SALES :		...	
AVERAGE COMMISSION :		...	

The rules for calculating the commission are :

SALES	**RATE**
<= 5000	2% of SALES
> 5,000 but <=20,000	3.5% of SALES
> 20,000 but <= 50,000	5% + Rs. 1,000
> 50,000	7% + Rs. 2,500

Develop the algorithm of the solution.

5.3. A company maintains inventory data in a file named ITEMFL. The master file is stored on part number and contains the following types of data for each item held in the inventory.

Field	**Data Type and Size**
Part number	5 numeric positions
Part name	15 alphanumeric positions
Quantity in stock	5 numeric positions

Another data file named TRANSFL contains records of transactions on the items in the inventory. Each record of this file consists of the following :

Field	**Data Type and Size**
Part number	5 numeric positions
Transaction code	1 numeric position
1 = receipt	
2 = issue	
Quantity transacted	5 numeric positions.

Draw a flowchart to show how the master file is updated on the basis of the records of the transaction file.

Develop an algorithm for the solution of the above problem.

5.4. A data file contains invoice records. The layout of the records is given below :

Field	Data Type and Size
Party code	5 alphanumeric
Invoice number	6 Numeric
Invoice data	6 (DD MM YY)
Gross value	7 Rs. & Paise
Discount amount	6 Rs. & Paise
Sales tax amount	7 Rs. & Paise
Net payable	7 Rs. & Paise

The records have been kept sorted in ascending sequence of Invoice Number.

It is required to accumulate totals of Gross value, Discount, Sales tax, and Net payable amounts, and print the totals.

Draw a flowchart showing the processing logic and write down the algorithm of the solution.

5.5. A credit bureau maintains a master file that lists for, each of its customers, a unique identification number, name, current principal that the customer owes, and his or her credit limit. The credit bureau also maintains a transaction file that tracks its customers' loans and payments. Each record in this file lists the customer's identification number, together with the transaction's amount and its date. A positive number indicates a payment and a negative number indicates a loan. Once a month the credit bureau updates its master file by processing entries in the transaction file. Assume that the master file records are sorted by identification number but the transaction file is not sorted.

Construct a flowchart and then develop the algorithm showing a program logic to update the master file.